SOCIAL
RESEARCH IN
COMMUNICATION
AND LAW

The SAGE CommText Series

Series Editor:
EVERETTE E. DENNIS
Gannett Center for Media Studies, Columbia University

Founding Editor: F. GERALD KLINE, *late of the School of Journalism and Mass Communication, University of Minnesota*

Founding Associate Editor: SUSAN H. EVANS, *Annenberg School of Communications, University of Southern California*

The **SAGE CommText** series brings the substance of mass communication scholarship to student audiences by blending syntheses of current research with applied ideas in concise, moderately priced volumes. Designed for use both as supplementary readings and as "modules" with which the teacher can "create" a new text, the **SAGE CommTexts** give students a conceptual map of the field of communication and media research. Some books examine topical areas and issues; others discuss the implications of particular media; still others treat methods and tools used by communication scholars. Written by leading researchers with the student in mind, the **SAGE CommTexts** provide teachers in communication and journalism with solid supplementary materials.

Available in this series:

Jeremy Cohen
Timothy Gleason

SOCIAL RESEARCH IN COMMUNICATION AND LAW

Volume 23　**The Sage CommText Series**

SAGE PUBLICATIONS
The Publishers of Professional Social Science
Newbury Park　London　New Delhi

TO OUR PARENTS,
Ruth and Ernest Cohen
and
James and Margaret Gleason

Copyright © 1990 by Sage Publications, Inc.

For information address:

SAGE Publications, Inc.
2111 West Hillcrest Drive
Newbury Park, California 91320

SAGE Publications Ltd.
28 Banner Street
London EC1Y 8QE
England

SAGE Publications India Pvt. Ltd.
M-32 Market
Greater Kailash I
New Delhi 110 048 India

Printed in the United States of America

Library of Congress Cataloging-in-Publication Data

Cohen, Jeremy, 1949-
    Social research in communication and law / Jeremy Cohen,
    Timothy Gleason.
        p. cm. — (The Sage commtext series ; 23)
    Includes bibliographical references.
    ISBN 0-8039-3266-9. — ISBN 0-8039-3267-7 (pbk.)
    1. Mass media — Law and legislation — United States. I. Gleason,
    Timothy W. II. Title. III. Series: Sage commtext series ; v. 23.
KF2750.C64 1990
343.7309'9 — dc20
[347.30399]   89-10732
                                                                  CIP

FIRST PRINTING, 1990

CONTENTS

FOREWORD

It is not unusual for legal scholars to study *communication law*, nor is it uncommon for communication and media scholars to study law and legal issues. But it is something of a departure for the two to commingle. Studies of law and communication with emphasis on law (especially media law) as a communication process have evident value to anyone who considers the intrinsic importance of these interrelated, but rarely explored concerns.

This is the mission that engages Jeremy Cohen and Timothy Gleason in *Social Research in Communication and Law* which makes a persuasive case for the interdisciplinary study of law and communication. To their research colleagues in the nation's communication and journalism schools they suggest that following the lead of law professors in publishing traditional law review articles about media law is not the way to go. Similarly, they urge scholars in other fields to move beyond a "sociology of law" approach wherein legal topics are simply fodder for research, as is religion, the family, or the school. While they do not deny the value of these studies, they believe that "communication and law" scholars can do something original that contributes to knowledge and, thus, to the public understanding of two symbiotic processes.

The mission that professors Cohen and Gleason outline provides a daunting challenge for students of communication law, history, and sociology. They have produced a book that is a valuable augmentation to courses by those names and for media ethics, issues, and problems in mass communication and several others. Students of communication law, criminal justice, judicial administration, and other fields will also benefit from reading and using this thoughtful book.

Although they don't say it bluntly, a subtext of this book is clearly a call for more rigorous work by students interested in the interface of communication and law. It is not enough, Cohen and Gleason posit, for a student of media law to work in isolation on one narrow legal specialty without a broader knowledge of jurisprudence and legal philosophy. Simi-

6

larly, those who study media law from a legal perspective ought to know more about the communication process and theoretical underpinnings.

Blessedly, this book is not a polemic nor a sermon, but rather a practical guide to doing research on law and communication questions. Along the way the authors offer rich citations and examples from the literature.

This book is a natural outgrowth of a current movement among communication law scholars to make more effective use of the methodologies of communication science. It is a stand against First Amendment reductionism which takes the researcher on a too easy path toward simple advocacy. Both authors have been active in that movement, although the book is a quite original step beyond social science applications in communication law. It is instead the confrontation of two substantive areas of knowledge with the scholarly tools of both as well as a few from related disciplines.

Social Research in Communication and Law appears at a time when we are experiencing a renaissance of interest in the interface of these vital social processes. Thoughtful readers will appreciate its message both in literal and more subtle ways.

—Everette E. Dennis
Series Editor

PREFACE AND ACKNOWLEDGMENTS

This book represents the authors' belief that freedom of expression is an area of research especially appropriate to the discipline of communication studies. Yet while freedom of expression may be anchored well within our discipline, understanding clearly requires familiarity with a variety of substantive fields and methodological approaches beyond the usual concerns of communication theory, such as legal studies, history, and jurisprudence.

Our approach is an interdisciplinary approach, which we refer to as *communication and law* to distinguish our concerns from traditional media law analyses harbored in case law and constitutional scholarship. This book is prefaced on the notion that communication researchers should not simply duplicate the efforts of legal scholars. A *communication and law* approach must distinguish itself from research generally recognized as within the traditional purview of law or legal studies. It should add to the literature of communication. It should be generated from the perspective of the communication scholar, not in competition with the legal scholar, but in recognition of the objectives of communication research.

This book is an attempt to encourage distinctions that recognize the relationships among communication theory, freedom of expression, history, and law and place them squarely within the identifiable domain of communication scholarship. Contextual understanding of communication and law can only benefit from familiarity with, and respect for, the integrity of each of these disciplines.

Throughout the preparation of these chapters the authors have shared, and benefited from, each other's ideas. The sum of the individual chapters is a shared approach and commitment to interdisciplinary social research in communication and law.

In fact, Jeremy Cohen holds principal responsibility for Chapters 1, 4, and 5. Timothy Gleason bears the primary responsibility for Chapters 2, 3, and 6. We accept equally the blame for whatever errors of thinking or fact are present.

We are grateful to a number of people for their encouragement, their criticism and their patience. Particular gratitude is due Everette Dennis at the Gannett Center for Media Studies at Columbia University, Richard Carter and Don Pember at the University of Washington, Arnold Ismach at the University of Oregon, Steven Chaffee at Stanford University, Jerilyn McIntyre and David Eason at the University of Utah, Al Gunther and Diana Mutz at the University of Wisconsin, and Vincent Price at the University of Michigan.

The Stanford Department of Communication lightened a teaching load and the University of Oregon Freshman Seminar Program and the School of Journalism provided much appreciated support. At Stanford, doctoral candidates Kathleen Kurz, Sara Spears, and Judy Polumbaum provided useful commentary. Gloria Beckwith untangled the mysteries of word processing and kept the phone at bay. Roni Holeton provided administrative support and continued encouragement and always found a way to make it possible to get in one more long-distance phone call, to secure one more needed journal and to make the project a lot easier on two authors living and working 500 miles apart.

Transaction Books provided gracious permission to quote Morris Cohen from his book of essays on law and legal philosophy, *Law and the Social Order*. We also appreciate permission to quote liberally from Sage Publications' *Handbook of Communication Science* by Charles Berger and Steven Chaffee.

And, of course, we are grateful for the love and encouragement of Jennifer Ulum, Catherine Jordan, and Leah and Joshua.

—Jeremy Cohen

—Timothy Gleason

1

PROBING COMMUNICATION AND LAW

Social research in communication and law requires the integration of two seemingly distinct disciplines that lay claim to numerous schools of research, methodology, and theory. Where law and communication maintain shared interests, such as in the study of freedom of expression, they invite new methods of study and observation and offer the potential for new perspective and theory.

Communication researchers interested in media law and freedom of expression require more than the ability to navigate the labyrinths of a law library, just as they must comprehend more than the application of a statistical analysis to legal phenomena. Legal scholars concerned with communication, too, have reason to consider the law in a context that goes beyond the narrow legal rule appropriate to adjudication and courtroom advocacy. Communication research involving law and legal questions is quite different from traditional legal research.

Too often, however, researchers specialize in communication *or* in law. Too rarely do individuals possess methodological and theoretical competency in both disciplines, probably because law and communication represent fundamentally different approaches to knowledge. Yet, if members of legal studies and communication research communities are to work with each other or simply understand each other's work, grounds must be prepared to make such a meeting possible.

More than a half century ago, legal scholar Roscoe Pound wrote, "Until some Anglo American jurist arises with the universal equipment of Joseph Kohler, the results of common-law incursions into philosophy will resemble the effort of the editorial writer who wrote upon Chinese metaphysics after reading in the *Encyclopedia Britannica* under China and metaphysics and then combining his information."[1] The rationale here is to provide communication scholars, whatever their primary research approach, with the ability to avoid encyclopedic approaches to integrated investigations involving communication and law. Legal scholars, too, should find the discussion a useful introduction to the concerns that drive communication research exploring freedom of expression, media law, and the interactions of communication and law.

CONCEPTUAL MAPS

This book is neither a text on how to conduct traditional legal research nor a guide to communication research methodologies. It is presented instead as a conceptual map of the emerging area of *communication and law*, which is, in turn, a means of raising basic questions about communication assumptions inherent in law. In doing so, there is a need to find suitable means for identifying those assumptions and for testing both their scientific and their legal validity. The research is at times *applied research*, as most of legal research has been. It is useful to use social research to challenge legal norms governing such areas as electronic news gathering in a courtroom, the prejudicial effects of pretrial publicity, and the influence of pornographic communications.

There is value in applied research that supplies the rounds for the volleys fired by attorneys prosecuting their cases. Trend surveys, studies of case law, predictions of judicial stances, and analyses of constitutional arguments play important roles in the development and understanding of normative, positivist law. As a practical matter, Wayne Newton's attorney included public opinion survey data in his 1987 libel suit against NBC.[2] The intent was to provide empirical proof that a series of television news broadcasts harmed the singer's reputation. The jury awarded $19 million in damages. After the trial Newton commissioned a second survey. This one purported to show a causal link between the size of the jury's award and the restoration of his positive public image. Does communication research bode greater fairness in the law with an increased ability to establish social facts? Or does the relative infancy of the field promise only smoke and mirrors and little substance in the courtroom for the foreseeable future?

Theoretical Value

Our primary concern, in any case, is with theory — with providing a means for *understanding* and for *explaining* communication and law rather than providing libel guidelines for journalists or courtroom strategies for defense and plaintiff attorneys. Before communication or legal scholars can operate effectively in an intellectual terrain influenced by both disciplines, however, some fundamental labors are in order. The first is to identify and explicate the differences among legal, communication, and philosophical theories of law; communication; and freedom of expression. Social scientists and legal advocates, after all, often seek differing ends and in turn have differing expectations for the use of theory.

Alone, neither the theories and attendant methodologies of communication nor of legal scholarship provide tools powerful enough to explain the full range of issues that exists within the study and practice of freedom of expression. Yet the fabrics of law and communication are too heavily interwoven to reasonably believe that we can ignore the tenets and postulates of one while trying to understand the other. The importance of expression in our constitutional framework and the prevalence and role of mass media subject to regulation in the civil courts, by administrative agency, and at times by criminal statute are daily reminders.

MERGING DISCIPLINES

There are of course dangers in the integrative process. It is easy to become snared in a trap that leaves social scientists calling for law based on the truths of their craft. The notion is hardly new. Roots can be found in the social engineering doctrines of the late 19th and early 20th centuries. Nor do the difficulties of reconciling theories from distinct disciplines end with the realization that while the social scientist analyzes libel as a concept requiring steadfast objectivity, the attorney views it as the object of a courtroom clash—the outcome of which is based on skills of unabashed, result-oriented advocacy.

The rational place to begin an interdisciplinary approach to communication and law is with the identification of freedom of expression as the common ground—yet mere recognition is hardly sufficient to generate theory that explains the complexity of the forces at work. We need to recognize and understand the variety of social concerns at play and the fundamental dichotomy between traditional legal and communication studies approaches.

The social research scholar—whether historian or communication scientist—is normally concerned with theory for its long-term value, not with how theory will be applied tomorrow in the legislature or the courthouse. Yet for many interested in freedom of expression, this is not entirely the case. First Amendment theory, for example, begins with a bias—the recognition of a compact among citizens that freedom and individual choice are preferable to an autocratic dictatorship. Many who conduct research in freedom of expression share this value. In communication and law we must recognize and respect the dichotomy that exists between communication scientists and legal theorists—and which may cause at least a mild case of schizophrenia in communication researchers.

CONSEQUENCES OF DECISION

Law is ultimately a set of normative constraints on human behavior. Some laws are simply based on decisions that certain behavior is unacceptable. Societies universally condemn murder, robbery, and fraud. Laws make such behaviors illegal and punishable, not based on any theory of how humans operate so much as on a belief that law provides an organized means for dealing with what we dislike. Other laws, such as those dealing with libel or sedition or pornography, are based on legal theories of why people will behave in manner X if exposed to condition Y. We fear a gullible and malleable public exposed to a bombardment of defamatory or politically or sexually provocative messages. It is quite logical to investigate this second type of law—often found in regulations involving freedom of expression—armed with both legal and communication theories.

Legal and communication theories are, indeed, different animals. The most obvious difference is one of function. Law is based on advocacy. The goal is to settle disputes and to regulate behavior. The judge faces the responsibility of the consequences of his decision. For the theorist, the arena is the journal rather than the courtroom. And while legal theory may indeed often originate within the academy, the scholar possesses the luxury of time unavailable to the judge. Parties to a law suit must concentrate on answerable questions that will lead to a win for one and a loss for the other. They must reach an answer. The law must provide the answer whatever the weaknesses in our understanding. And the time allotted to reach an answer is finite. Communication researchers, on the other hand, need not have immediate answers. They may ask questions with no thought of winners and losers, judgments and verdicts, or appeals and settlements.

COMMUNICATION AND LAW

Social research in communication and law, then, involves the integration of two, seemingly distinct, disciplines that in turn lay claim to numerous schools of research and theory. While one researcher applies scientific inquiry to the processes and effects of communication, another develops a juristic "logic" that unabashedly slants the evidence to fit the legal cause advocated. Their methods, goals, and operational rules differ fundamentally, yet both are well within the norms of their respective disciplines.

Researchers arrive at an intersection of interests where law is based on behavioral and social assumptions about communication. Libel law, for example, balances the value of unabated speech against the destruction of personal reputation. The libel tort encompasses the belief that defamatory untruths have the power to alter significantly public attitudes and opinions about individuals. Despite the inherent overlap of communication and law, however, the legal scholar focuses almost exclusively on the attorney's advocacy and shaping of legal theory to meet the client's needs, and the acceptance or rejection of those arguments by the courts. The communication scientist, meanwhile, may investigate the processes and effects of the defamatory expression on public opinion, without attending to the judicial encounters that drive the dispute. Combining the study of law and communication is not as simple as recognizing that the two disciplines share some common conceptual interests.

Social research in *communication and law* implies inquiry that goes beyond traditional jurisprudential case analysis by recognizing the structure of jurisprudence and examining that structure with tools and theory normally associated with communication science, historiography, and critical studies — the traditional tools of the communication scholar.

This book is intended to bridge the conceptual and methodological canyons that separate the disciplines — law and communication — when they are seen as distinct. In many senses, law and communication are unique fields. Yet where they maintain shared interests, such as in the study of freedom of expression, the fields invite new methods of study and observation and offer the potential for new perspective. We are interested not simply in studying law *and* in studying communication, but in studying *law and communication*, a combination meant to suggest an awareness of the relation between the two fields as well as the offerings and limitations of each.

CONTEXT

The focus of this book is social research in communication and law. It is the result of both interest and frustration. The interest is in freedom of expression which carries the question, how should freedom of expression be studied? There is, of course, no single answer. Understanding requires context. How are expression and thought affected by regulation? How do institutions and economic systems encourage or interfere with freedom of expression? How do sociological ebbs and flows and historical currents play upon the course of expression and freedom? Scholars and students may study First Amendment theory, case law, or legal and social history. Journalism and mass communication professors Donald Gillmor and Everette Dennis wrote,

> Law, like history, is an area of *substantive knowledge*, but legal scholarship is also linked to specific *legal research methodologies*. Confusion increases when you realize that studies of legal issues and problems in mass communication (or in other fields, for that matter) also lend themselves to a variety of other methodological approaches. The methods of history, philosophy, sociology and other disciplines have been applied to the law for many years.[3]

The frustration is the result of attempts to apply to communication law methodologies appropriate to other disciplines in a helter-skelter fashion. It is tempting for social researchers to view communication law through the eyes of their own field. The practice, however, is fraught with peril when the attempt is made without fully understanding the processes and practices of law. It is a little like attempting to translate a French newspaper with a Japanese dictionary. Both French and Japanese are languages, but the rules of one do not apply to the other.

In fact, legal scholars have been interested in social research for nearly a century. Historians credit the first successful use of social research in the courts to Louis Brandeis in *Muller v. Oregon* (1908).[4] At issue was an Oregon statute forbidding women from working more than 10 hours per day. Brandeis presented the Court with a brief that included a collection of social, economic, and public health research on the theory that "[legal] propositions are not considered abstractly, but always with reference to facts."[5]

On the other hand, eight decades after *Muller*, law professor Geoffrey Hazzard framed the issue of applying social research to law in pragmatic terms hardly appreciative of Brandeis' pioneering work:

> In the end, as against the exigencies of the law's processes, the uses of behavioral science are relatively remote, its methods relatively expensive, and its results relatively inconsequential. Its findings are, of course, more satisfying to the modern mind than the conclusions advanced from authority. That, however, is not much consolation for law men, whose concerns are for immediate, cheap, and significant decision making. For them, there are continuing attractions to the Delphic Oracle.[6]

Hazzard's conclusions have some validity in day-to-day courtroom skirmishes where advocacy, rather than scientific truth, is the currency of success. His warning should cause social scientists anxious to fit their methods to law to pause and to consider the purposes of their quest. Few areas *appear* to offer greater support for skepticism over the practical fit between social science theory and legal practice. They can indeed appear to be separated by unbridgeable chasms.

SOCIAL RESEARCH IN THE COURTS

Fortunately, the driving force behind this book is not the need for immediate, cheap, and significant decision making. Rather, the goal is to more fully understand communication and law. The reward is heuristic. The bonus is the knowledge that on occasion, law does in fact take into consideration the work of the social scientist. *Brown v. Board of Education* (1954),[7] a controversial and landmark school desegregation case, considered the issue of whether the segregationist racial policy of "separate but equal" practiced by many school districts violated the 14th Amendment. Aided by social research findings that separating black school children from white children caused serious learning inequities for black youngsters, the Supreme Court was able to reverse legal precedent entrenched since *Plessy v. Ferguson* (1896).[8] *Plessy*, the law of the land for 58 years, was a 19th-century railroad case in which the Court upheld the constitutionality of a law "that all railway companies carrying passengers in their coaches in the State [of Louisiana] shall provide equal but separate accommodations for the white and colored races."[9]

Chandler v. Florida (1981) is a case more familiar to First Amendment students.[10] The defendants, two off-duty policemen arrested while trying to rob a restaurant, launched a 14th Amendment due process challenge to Florida's practice of allowing broadcast coverage of trials. The Court took pains to point out that although the case dealt with the claim of a constitutional ban on allowing cameras in the courtroom, it was a 14th Amendment case, not a First Amendment issue. In the end, after taking notice of social research into the psychological effects of the presence of cameras in the courtroom, the Court ruled that the Constitution neither requires, nor bans, such coverage. The Court's awareness of the social research evidence was an important element.

In fact, a 1978 study of Supreme Court decisions reported that in roughly one third of 601 cases examined, "the justices resorted to identifiable social science materials, although these were not necessarily crucial to the *ratio decidendi* in a case."[11] Those who practice law, or who must understand it because they undertake various practices, such as journalism, that are at times regulated by law, dwell within a context quite different from that occupied by those who approach law from an academic vista. Nonetheless, the full panorama can be eye-opening to all who are concerned with freedom of expression, whatever their academic or professional bias.

DO WE HAVE A DISTINGUISHABLE DISCIPLINE?

The thesis which drives this discussion is our belief that a thorough understanding of the *concept* and *practice* of freedom of expression is greatly enhanced by close familiarity with the *disciplines* of communication and law. We do not distinguish in our discussions among freedom of expression, freedom of speech, and freedom of the press. While there are important concepts within such distinctions, we use the terms somewhat interchangeably. Freedom of expression, then, is affected by laws that have an impact upon the behavior of individuals. The behavioral element brings the issue well within the discipline of communication research. Similarly, numerous laws and legal practices are based on assumptions about relationships between communication and behavior. Again, this suggests that the researcher schooled in communication may be able to add unique perspective and understanding to the interactions of law, communication, and freedom of expression.

The intent here is not to define the substantive discipline of communication. Rather it is to recognize the relationships among freedom of expression and communication and law. Attorneys or journalism teachers may well be able to complete their task satisfactorily by understanding the black letter law office analysis of case law. Scholars and students who want to go beyond industrial training; who want to understand the forces that push and pull on freedom of expression; who want to go beyond the narrow boundaries of normative law must, however, have a substantive understanding of freedom of expression *and* communication *and* law. This, then, is a call for an interdisciplinary approach to freedom of expression that takes into account the unique functions, theories, and methods of communication and law to explore the concept and practice of freedom of expression.

It is also a call to an issue of first order importance in a field as young as communication studies. Can we identify and develop research parameters that distinguish social research in *communication and law* from the territory already well staked out by the legal scholar or the constitutional historian? Do we in fact have a discipline, or are we simply aping the research already carried on in scores of law schools? We believe the sum of the parts is greater than the whole — that by using an interdisciplinary approach that borrows from communication, law, history, and other disciplines, the researcher in *communication and law* works within a unique and distinguishable subdiscipline of communication studies.

GOALS

Beyond the identification of concept and practice we are seeking the ability to comment upon and *to generate* theory. As scholars interested in *communication and law* we are interested in legal theory. We are interested in communication theory. We are interested in theories of freedom of expression. From the discipline of *communication and law* we should be able to generate theory that is cognizant of and realistic about law, communication, and freedom of expression — an integrated theory, if you will, predicated on the relationships among law, communication, and freedom of expression.

Must such work be immediately applicable to a courtroom or brief? Isn't it likely that many judges are unlikely to accept such work? The answer is basic — although it will receive more comment later on in Chapter 5. Our discipline is communication. Our research interests theoretical as well as policy-oriented. Kurt Lewin's aphorism remains useful: "There is nothing so practical as a good theory."

It also seems useful to establish at the outset a secondary intent. There is a tendency to use interchangeably the labels *communication and law* and *social science and law*. For a number of years, the Association for Education in Journalism and Mass Communication, for example, has held panels on social science and law. Communication is a discipline in the social sciences. Our interest here, though, is not the social sciences in general. Our intent is to focus on the specific discipline called communication. We are not so much interested in the application of social science methodologies as we are in the potential for theory available from scientific discipline and other methodological approaches found in communication studies.

The usually lax use of communication and social science as synonymous terms within the legal context has led more than a few researchers to believe that by applying the quantitative tools of the social scientist they are practicing communication research. Experimental design and survey research are tools used by the communication scientist, but their presence alone is no guarantee that we are traveling in the land of communication. Psychologists, physicists, demographers, geographers, and White House spokesmen also use statistical analyses—all without ever contributing to our understanding of communication. For our intents and purposes social science—the study of which includes a broad range of methodological tools—refers to the study of social relations. We are interested here not in social relations in general, but in the relations found specifically within the context of communication and law.

Our primary intent is to cover three issues:

1) The theoretical and methodological elements that distinguish among law, freedom of expression, and communication and the conceptual approaches needed to bridge these disciplines.
2) The validation (or invalidation) of assumptions about communication embedded in law.
3) The use of social research to identify and examine the impact of law on communication.

WHERE WE ARE GOING

Let's take these one at a time. Our goals deal with *ways of knowing and thinking*; with the processes and effects of communication on an *individual level of analysis*; and with the processes and effects of communication on a *societal level of analysis*, a micro and a macro approach if you will.

Chapters 2, 3, 4, and 5 each focus on our first goal, which is to understand the difference between law, freedom of expression, and communication. These chapters establish not only the difficulty of applying social research to law, but the reasoning behind that difficulty. At the heart of this discussion are the differing—perhaps competing—functions of theory and methodology in communication and in law.

The function of Chapter 2 is to provide an understanding of what we mean by law and a brief introduction to legal theory and legal structure sufficient to alert the communication researcher to the requirements of conducting social research in law.

Chapter 3 introduces readers to the dominant theoretical constructions developed by the courts and by legal commentators and develops the conceptual difference between freedom of expression and law.

In Chapter 4 we will look at some research in libel that exemplifies the value of interdisciplinary social research.

Chapter 5 focuses on communication studies as a discipline and examines the conceptual traps awaiting the researcher who attempts to integrate law and communication. We also take notice here of the role of values in communication and law.

Chapter 6 is a summing up and provides the opportunity for discussion. Alternative research approaches focusing on social research methodologies are only now emerging as active disciplines for communication scholars and students interested in law. It has become clear that communication researchers interested in media law and freedom of expression benefit from contextual research approaches that not only predict the legal outcome likely to follow certain fact situations, but which strive to explain the collision of unabated expression and regulation. As the interests of communication scientists, social researchers, and legal scholars continue to merge under the general heading of communication studies, the need for an integrated approach becomes increasingly apparent.

We close Chapter 6 with some thoughts about where social research in communication and law might take us and about freedom of expression theory that takes into account law and communication.

NOTES

1. Roscoe Pound, *An Introduction to the Philosophy of Law* (New Haven, 1922): viii.

2. United States District Court, District of Nevada, Case No. CV-LV-81-180, MDC (1987), *unreported*.

3. Donald M. Gillmor and Everette E. Dennis, "Legal Research in Mass Communication," in Guido H. Stempel III and Bruce Westley, eds., *Research Methods in Mass Communication* (Englewood Cliffs, N.J., 1981): 320.

4. Muller v. Oregon, 208 U.S. 412 (1908).

5. Ronald K. Collins and Jennifer Friesen, "Looking Back on Muller v. Oregon," *American Bar Association Journal* 69 (1983): 294.

6. Geoffrey C. Hazzard, Jr., "Limitations on the Uses of Behaviorial Science in the Law," *CASE Western Law Review* 19 (1987): 76–7.

7. Brown v. Board of Education of Topeka, 347 U.S. 483 (1954).

8. Plessy v. Ferguson, 163 U.S. 537 (1896).

9. Ibid., 540.

10. Chandler v. Florida, 449 U.S. 560 (1981).

11. Henry J. Abraham, *The Judicial Process* (New York, 1980): 248.

2

AN INTRODUCTION TO LAW AND LEGAL THEORY

A researcher working in the law requires an understanding of legal concepts, theories, conventions, and rules. In addition, the researcher should be aware of the influence of legal culture and legal scholarship. The law of freedom of expression, as is the case with all laws, is the result of the interplay of complex influences that must be considered both individually and together.

Freedom of expression is generally viewed as a legal concept and it is defined in legal terms, but too frequently nonlegal researchers enter the legal domain without full recognition of the importance of understanding the law.

In the effort to draw broader meaning from legal documents or to make comprehensible to a larger audience the sometimes arcane writings of lawyers and judges, researchers ignore or misconstrue the *legal* meaning and significance of documents and evidence. Without a clear concept of what law is and of the language and data of law, the interdisciplinary researcher is likely to produce material that is at best irrelevant and at worst just plain wrong.

A researcher attempting to study "First Amendment" questions might well heed legal historian Morton Horwitz's advice. A legal researcher "is brought face to face with the problems of being faithful to the internal technical structure of a discipline while at the same time providing a more general perspective from which to measure its significance."[1]

It is tempting to dismiss legal technicalities as being important only to lawyers, but to do so is to ignore elements of the law central to understanding the discipline. Just as a reader must understand the theories, rules, and conventions of statistics in order to make sense of a statistical analysis, a reader of a court's opinion must understand the nature and structure of laws to make use of legal materials.

Danger arises because the statistically ignorant reader is confronted with an inaccessible text, while the novice reader of a judicial opinion, a no less complicated and specialized document, finds a seemingly accessible (although frequently deadly) text. A complex set of legal rules, constraints, and conventions gives meaning to legal writing. Without a grounding in the law, a reader of legal documents will not understand the significance of the material under review.

The case of *Snepp v. United States* (1980) illustrates the danger. The case raises an important First Amendment question about government's power to restrain the speech of government employees and has since been used as a precedent for attempts to expand the government's use of contractual agreements limiting the free speech rights of employees.[2] However, the litigation pivots on narrowly drawn questions of contract law and damages, not on the constitutional guarantee of freedom of speech and press.

Frank Snepp, a former employee of the Central Intelligence Agency, had signed a prepublication review agreement as a condition of employment when he joined the CIA. The agreement prohibited publication of any information learned during or as a result of his CIA employment without prepublication review by the Agency.

Snepp published a book about the CIA without review. The book did not contain any classified information. The CIA sued him for *breach of contract*. A federal district court held that Snepp had violated his contract with the CIA, enjoined violation of the contract as to further works, and ruled that all royalties from Snepp's book must be placed in a "constructive trust" to be turned over to the CIA.[3]

The court of appeals affirmed the trial court's ruling on the breach of contract question, but overturned the establishment of the constructive trust. It said that a jury could award punitive damages to the government for the violation of the contract, but that the constructive trust theory was not available.[4]

On appeal to the Supreme Court, Snepp argued that prepublication review was an unconstitutional prior restraint of his right to speak and therefore a violation of the First Amendment. A divided Supreme Court rejected his First Amendment claim. The majority reasoned that Snepp had voluntarily signed the agreement and that the secrecy requirements of the contract were reasonable given the nature of the CIA's "mandate to 'protect intelligence sources and methods from unauthorized disclosure.' "

The dissenters argued that the CIA's suppression of Snepp's book went beyond any legitimate secrecy interest since the book did not contain any state secrets, and that no legal authority existed to support the funneling of Snepp's royalties into a constructive trust.[5]

Snepp is a "First Amendment case." Its effect is to establish clear government authority to use contractual gag orders to restrain the speech of government employees where national security interests are implicated. The Supreme Court rejected the claim that the First Amendment prohibits this form of prior restraint.

But why did the majority reject the free press position? The case has First Amendment implications, but it was decided largely on other legal grounds. In order to fully understand the decision, several other aspects of the case must be considered: the use of the theories, rules, and principles of contract law; the importance the justices appear to have placed on the fact that Snepp had voluntarily entered into an agreement which he then broke; and the history of judicial deference to national security claims (in spite of the "preferred position" of the First Amendment). The researcher examining the *Snepp* decision must take into account all of the legal factors found in the case before reaching a conclusion about its significance to the law of freedom of the press.

The Use of Social Research in the Law

Lack of understanding of the legal system not only leads to misunderstanding of legal documents, but it also leads to misdirected research efforts. The legal definition of "actual malice" and the evidentiary requirements (i.e., the evidence a plaintiff must present to prove actual malice) of that requirement illustrate the difficulty.

The definition of actual malice in libel law has little in common with the general understanding of "malice" and is significantly different from the common law definitions of malice as either "ill will" or "intentionally harming someone."

In *New York Times v. Sullivan* (1964), the Supreme Court defined actual malice as "knowledge of falsity" or "reckless disregard for the truth."[6] Four years later, in *St. Amant v. Thompson* (1968), the Court held that proving actual malice was not simply a matter of determining if the defendant had been reckless in efforts to verify the truth of a story. In addition, the "state of mind" of the defendant had to be considered. The Court said that there "must be sufficient evidence to permit the conclusion that the defendant in fact entertained serious doubts as to the truth of his publication."[7] The evidence must show that the defendant had serious doubt about the truth, not merely that the story was slanted, biased, or unfair.

In a recent libel case brought by a bulk meat retailer against the ABC program *20/20* for a story titled "Bum Steer," the plaintiff hired Marilyn A. Lashner, a communication researcher, to testify on the question of evidence of actual malice or — as it is sometimes called — constitutional malice. The expert witness compared the transcripts of "Bum Steer" to 11 outtakes (unedited videotapes of interviews) from the story.

She assumed that the outtakes represented a "standard of objectivity" and analyzed the transcripts for "linguistic neutrality" and "evenhandedness." The researcher found that "ABC intentionally acted in a negative and biased manner, showed reckless disregard for the substance and tone of information that was presented to them by outside sources, and failed in its newsgathering procedures to exercise due care toward obtaining information about plaintiff that was valid, reliable, and free from errors."

The trial court did not challenge the validity of the research; however, it concluded that "the First Amendment requires more of a libel plaintiff than can be demonstrated by this limited approach." In other words, while the "evaluative assertion analysis" performed might be valid it did not address the *legal* requirements in the case.[8] Examining the product of newsgathering might demonstrate biased reporting, but it does not show the "state of mind" of the reporters and editors at ABC.

The purpose of this chapter is not to provide sufficient background in the law for legal research. That task is far beyond the scope of this book. Nor is it our intention to introduce the structural nuts and bolts of the American legal system. That information is readily available elsewhere. Here we present a basic guide to the study of law by introducing some of the larger issues that confront a researcher working in the legal domain. The chapter addresses the nature of law, the importance of legal process, and the legal culture. Finally it discusses the influence of different schools of legal scholarship on the understanding of the law.

Each of the areas addressed presents questions for students of law and communication. While all the questions cannot be answered in a chapter, if researchers enter the legal domain aware of the issues discussed here, many of the pitfalls of interdisciplinary research in the law can be avoided.

LEGAL THEORY

Theory provides a means for making sense of a chaotic world. All good theory distinguishes differences, but theory is not the same across disciplines. Scientists develop theory to "make sense of what would otherwise be inscrutable or unmeaning empirical findings."[9] Lawyers, philosophers, and others concerned with developing legal theory do so in order to establish *proper* frameworks for ordering society.

The lines between legal theory, political theory, and philosophy are blurred (at least one author sees no distinction; he refers to "Legal philosophy or theory").[10] Legal theorists are concerned with normative, not empirical, standards. Law professor John Finch describes legal theory as "a study of the characteristic features essential to law and common to legal systems. One of its chief objects is the analysis of the basic elements of law which make it law and distinguish it from other forms of rules or standards."[11]

Where the scientist uses theory for the purpose of explaining and understanding observed conditions, the legal scholar uses legal theory to prescribe conditions that *ought* to exist in a legal system. "Legal theory," Finch writes, "deals with questions as to the nature of law. As such, it is more concerned with an analysis of the character of law or of a legal system than with an exposition of its content, the specific regulations themselves."[12]

The test of legal theory is not the ability of a theory to withstand empirical testing, but rather, the ability of a given theory to "explain the function, the practical point of the various aspects and components of law and legal systems, so as to show why there is a good practical reason for these aspects and components to cluster together as a distinct social enterprise."[13]

Central to the task of the legal theorist is the effort to develop theories of law in order, as law professor Philip Soper wrote, "to understand the existing connections between such basic concepts as justice, law, authority, and obligation."[14]

What Is Law?

H.L.A. Hart, one of the most influential legal philosophers of the 20th century, began *A Concept of Law* (1961), a pivotal work defining his view of positive law, with the observation that "Few questions concerning human society have been asked and answered by serious thinkers in so many diverse, strange, and even paradoxical ways as the question 'What is law?' "[15]

This seemingly simple question continues to defy an easy answer. We all know law when we see it. We stop at red lights because it is the law. But the legal theorist is asking a much more complicated question: What are the understandings which shape and give force to the rules a society recognizes as law? Law performs many functions in a society. To define law is to attempt to find a statement that encompasses all the functions of law: from regulating traffic to constitutional protections of individual rights such as freedom of the press.

The function of law goes beyond the regulation of behavior; it also "provides a process through which we create a social identity, by which we reflect and embody the aspirations and values of the community."[16] Law as a shaper of national identity is particularly relevant to the question of freedom of the press in the United States. The strong American tradition of belief in and advocacy of freedom of the press as an individual right and a check on government power plays an important role in defining a sense of national identity in the United States. In U.S. history the tradition has generally exceeded the actual legal limits or tolerance of freedom of expression, but the tradition is central to concepts of individualism in the United States.[17]

This complexity of functions makes it difficult to define law. Law is far more complex than a simple definition of "That which must be obeyed." Law professor Karl Llewellyn once observed that "The difficulty in framing any concept of law is that there are so many things to be included, and the things to be included are so unbelievably different from each other."[18]

One working definition of law is "the enterprise of subjecting human conduct to the governance of rules." Another is "a system of authoritative and prescriptive rules of conduct and as a process of dispute resolution via the application of these rules in adjudication."[19] Both definitions describe law, but neither addresses the normative question at the center of most discussions of legal theory. What constitutes a *valid* or *good* law? This is essentially a question about the moral content of law. Or, to raise a classic question of late 20th-century legal theory: Did Germany under Nazi rule have a valid legal system?

Natural Law or Legal Positivism?

What characteristics make a rule a valid law? If citizens obey a rule merely because a powerful government compels obedience, is the rule part of a valid legal system? These questions are at the heart of an ongoing debate in legal theory between advocates of *natural law theory* and *legal positivism*.

Natural law theorists judge the validity of positive law (i.e., laws created by members of a society) against a set of rules grounded in something more fundamental than the conventions or customs of humankind. Natural law is based on assumptions about the rationality and intelligence of humans and the existence of a higher rational order of things.[20] Hart described the conventional view of natural law as "certain principles of human conduct, awaiting discovery by human reason, with which man made law must conform if it is to be valid."[21] If positive law is in conflict with the higher natural law, then the positive law is invalid.

In contrast, legal positivists argue that law can exist independently of any moral content, although it frequently reflects the moral values of society. Positivists hold that law consists of preexisting standards identified by origins and sources. For the classic legal positivist, sanctions are the sufficient characteristic of law. If a rule is the command of a sovereign whom the populace habitually obeys then it is a law, regardless of its moral content or validity. A classical positivist definition of law is, "A set of definite rules of human conduct with appropriate sanctions for their enforcement, both of these being prescribed by duly constituted human authority."[22]

International law presents the best example of the contrast. From a natural law perspective, the set of rules agreed upon by nations to regulate international conduct are laws because they are based on agreed upon moral principles. A document such as the *United Nations Declaration on Human Rights* is law because it is in agreement with principles of human conduct. However, to the legal positivist, the UN declaration is law only if it carries legal sanction. Its source of authority could not be solely a principle of human rights. Without a set of enforceable sanctions, the UN declaration is not a law.

The distinction between natural and positive law is important to interdisciplinary research because law in the United States is grounded in legal positivism. Appeals are made to natural law and fundamental rights, and the importance of natural law theory in the development of American law cannot be ignored, but such appeals do not carry the *force* of law. They are not determinative in defining the meaning of law.

In looking at First Amendment questions, the role of legal positivism in answering the question "what is law" raises critical issues about the nature and meaning of constitutional protection of freedom of expression. In a positive law tradition, freedom of expression is defined by legislative acts and judicial rulings. Freedom of expression, to borrow Justice Charles Evans Hughes' phrase, "is what the judges [and the legislators] say it is."[23]

As will be discussed later, natural law theories play an important role in shaping the positive law of freedom of the press. Claims of "First Amendment rights" are powerful because of the strong tradition of fundamental individual rights in the United States. But it is important to keep in mind that the tradition of freedom of the press in the United States is far broader than is the positive law protection of the right to freedom of the press.

RIGHTS

Ronald Dworkin, an important late 20th-century legal philosopher, has observed that "the language of rights now dominates political debate in the United States."[24] The question, "What is a right?" has generated as much, if not more, discussion and debate as the effort to define the nature and meaning of law. The distinction between natural rights and legal rights parallels the distinction between natural law and legal positivism.

In no area of politics and law is this truer than in the area of mass media law. The cry of a "First Amendment *right*" is heard in debates and litigation ranging across the free press landscape, from challenges to national security prior restraints to attempts to stop city zoning regulations requiring television stations to place all transmitting antennae on a single tall building. What does it mean to assert a right to freedom of the press?

Rights are generally viewed as an individual's claim against the government. The existence of a right either requires the government to act on the individual's behalf or prohibits the government from interfering with the exercise of an individual right. The classic view of freedom of the press in the United States is that the individual has the right to speak without fear of government censorship or punishment. The claim of a right to freedom of the press resonates throughout the history of the United States, yet the claim is not self-defining.

The speech and press clauses of the First Amendment are part of the Bill of Rights to the U.S. Constitution. Freedom of speech and press—along with freedom of religion, assembly, and petition—makes up the First Amendment component of the bundle of rights viewed as fundamental to liberty under the Constitution. But few have considered these rights absolute. Instead, they must be interpreted to determine their scope. No one would argue seriously that freedom of the press is not a fundamental right, but significant debate exists over the proper limits of the right to freedom of the press—that is, the limits established by positive law.

The First Amendment theories used to sort out the disagreement over positive limits are discussed in detail in Chapter 3. Here we want to illustrate the important difference between the principle of freedom of the press as a fundamental right and the difficulty in translating that principle into positive law. The point is that all free expression rights are not the same. The central questions asked concern the nature of rights: (1) What is the source of the right? (2) Is it an individual right or a collective right?

The Source of Rights

Natural law requires that humans have freedom of expression and that it is an absolute and inalienable right. However, the history of freedom of speech and press demonstrates the uncertainty of the defined limits of the rights. On this question, natural rights theory provides little guidance.

In the realm of positive law, the claim of a natural right is accepted as part of the tradition and custom of American law. Few would argue that a natural right of freedom of expression doesn't exist, and some would bring the natural right claim to bear when attempting to interpret constitutional protections, but in positivist terms the natural right claim is not determinative. The determinative question is the meaning of the positive right of freedom of the press found in state constitutions and the Bill of Rights in the Federal Constitution.

From a positivist legal perspective, the sources of protection of freedom of the press are state and federal constitutions, legislative acts, and administrative rules that are in agreement with constitutional free expression provisions and the common law. These sources create rules and definitions for legal protection of freedom of the press.

This is a question of limits. The task is not to determine whether a right exists, but rather to determine the limits of the positive right of freedom of the press. In contrast to the absolute natural right to freedom of expression, positive rights are by definition limited. There are no absolute positive rights!

This process is frequently described as a "line drawing" or a "balancing" process. Courts and legislatures must define the limits of positive rights at points where rights appear to be in conflict. In free press law the long and ongoing struggle to draw appropriate boundaries between, for example, the perceived conflict between the constitutional rights to freedom of the press and a fair trial, or the right of freedom of the press and the perceived harmful effects of pornographic speech suggest the complexity of the problems confronted in defining the limits of positive rights.

Contrary to a widely-held popular view of the right to freedom of the press, the history of interpretation of state and federal protection of freedom of the press is not a story of strong, broad protection of expression. Until the 20th century, constitutional guarantees protected a relatively narrow range of expression. Harvard law professor Laurence Tribe describes the history of the First Amendment as one that "has waxed and waned with the political tides. . . . In short, the constitutional axiom of free expression has been only slightly more immune to the pressures of politics, culture, and the marketplace than any other aspect of our laws."[25]

Much of the struggle described as "balancing" is not simply an objective search for a neutral judgment, but rather disagreement over fundamental questions about the nature of political systems and the relation of individuals to society. It is a debate about the nature of rights.

Individual Right or Public Good?

The difference in the level of protection for expression can be explained by changing views of the nature of the right. Prior to the 20th century, the public good served by the content of speech determined the limits of the right to freedom of expression. If expression disturbed the public order, it fell outside free expression protections. Political science professor John Roche found, in his study of civil liberties in the United States, that "the whole notion of individual rights *enforceable against the community* . . . is a twentieth century legal innovation."[26]

Nineteenth-century jurists saw no contradiction between legal protection of freedom of the press and state laws prohibiting the publication of "crime news." In the eyes of legislators and judges the publication of such material served no public good and therefore banning such speech did not violate the freedom of the press. Until *Near v. Minnesota* (1931), when the Supreme Court held that a Minnesota state law allowing the state to restrain newspapers found to be public nuisances violated the First Amendment, the free press clause did not prevent state actions of this sort.[27]

The power of constitutional protection of freedom of the press is in terms of the law a recent development. In the 20th century, we have developed a strong protection of freedom of the press grounded in a concept of freedom of the press as an *individual* right.

This concept of right creates higher barriers against government restraints on speech. Instead of evaluating the public good of speech, it assumes an inherent value in speech to both the individual and to society. This assumption creates a strong claim against government. In order to overcome the individual's right to speak, the government must show a compelling interest in stopping the speech. The individual right of freedom of the press dominates some areas of 20th-century free press case law but a close look reveals that individual right and public good concepts of freedom of the press exist side-by-side in mass media law. The contrast is clearest when the First Amendment rights of broadcasters and newspaper publishers are compared.

Individual Versus Societal Rights

In *Red Lion Broadcasting v. FCC* (1969), the Supreme Court heard a challenge to the Fairness Doctrine and the equal time rule. Under Federal Communication Commission rules, broadcasters were required to provide access to television and radio stations to speakers with competing points of view. The Supreme Court held that the FCC's regulations were constitutional. The Court distinguished print media from broadcast media on the basis of technological differences. More important, the Court located the basis of broadcasters' right to speak with the *audience* in *Red Lion*: "We see the government controlling broadcast communication because of the *paramount right of the viewers and listeners to this limited medium* [italics added]."[28]

In 1974, in *Miami Herald Publishing Co. v. Tornillo*, the Court heard a challenge to a Florida state law requiring newspapers to provide free equal space for political candidates who had been attacked in a newspaper. Here the Court relied on an individual right concept of freedom of the press to hold that the statute violated the First Amendment:

> Even if a newspaper would face no additional costs to comply with a compulsory access law and would not be forced to forego publication of news or opinion by the inclusion of a reply, the Florida statute fails to clear the barriers of the First Amendment *because of its intrusion into the function of editors* [italics added]. The choice of material to go into a newspaper, and the decisions made as to limitations on the size and content of the paper, and the treatment of public issues and public officials . . . constitute the exercise of editorial control and judgment. It has yet to be demonstrated how governmental regulation of this crucial process can be exercised consistent with First Amendment guarantees of a free press as they have evolved to this time.[29]

The First Amendment standards in *Red Lion* and *Miami Herald* can be distinguished on the differences between print and broadcast technologies, but that distinction does not explain the two concepts of the right to freedom of expression found in the cases. On the level of rights, the cases can be understood only if the difference between the individual-based right used in *Miami Herald* and the public-good-based right in *Red Lion* is recognized.

Once that difference is identified, it is possible to sort out the different claims made in the current debate over the regulation of broadcasting and new technologies. When broadcasters call for "full First Amendment rights" or cable system operators claim to be more like newspapers than like television, the real conflict is over the meaning of the First Amendment right to freedom of expression. Is it a right belonging to individual speakers? Is it a right belonging to the public because of the unique characteristics of a particular information delivery system? Before the limits of the right can determined, the nature of the right must be defined.[30]

LEGAL SYSTEM

A legal system is a "problem solving machine."[31] It is a means of channeling behavior to conform to societal norms for resolving disputes between government and individuals and among individuals. This role is most obvious when two parties come before a court with competing claims as to the correct settlement of a dispute. But at all levels, from the elected executive who evokes a law to deliver disaster aid to drought-stricken farmers, to the legislature that passes a law requiring motorcycle riders to wear helmets, to the state supreme court that finds as a matter of law that the phrases "you're crooked" and "you crooked bastard" are not actionable libelous statements,[32] the law provides structure and process for controlling behavior and resolving disputes. As in any system involving human behavior, activity within the system is influenced by process and structure. The results of the system — in this instance the law — cannot be understood fully unless the influence of the system is taken into account.

An understanding of legal structure and process is important for the interdisciplinary researcher because legal disputes are always influenced and sometimes decided by the demands of structure and process.

Primary and Secondary Rules

Hart divided the law into two types of rules, primary rules and secondary rules. Primary rules are "concerned with the actions that individuals must or must not do"; that is, they are the substance of law. The press clause of the First Amendment is a primary rule; it limits the power of Congress to abridge the right to publish.

Secondary rules "specify the ways in which the primary rules may be conclusively ascertained, introduced, eliminated, varied, and the fact of their violation conclusively determined." Secondary laws establish the rules of legal practice. These rules have a significant influence in shaping substantive law.[33]

A large portion of a law student's course of study and subsequent practice of law is occupied with mastery of secondary rules. Rules of jurisdiction, pleading, evidence, administrative law, and a host of other sets of rules establish the way in which a legal question is to be pursued.

Communication questions concerning the litigation process or the results of litigation illustrate the importance of secondary rules. Researchers interested in examining the communication behavior of trial participants, the communication assumptions found in the law, or the results of litigation are entering an extremely constricted forum. Rather than assume rational or reasonable communication behaviors, researchers must look to the secondary rules regulating behavior before constructing research models.

For example, jury instructions raised questions about the ability of jurors to understand complex verbal information and about the ways in which jurors interpret evidence. Jurors are subjected to long and complicated instructions from the judge—in libel cases the reading of instructions can take more than a full day—as to how they are to interpret evidence introduced at trial. While the legal instructions may agree with accepted research models, it is more often the case that jurors are instructed to interpret information in ways that either are in conflict or at least disagreement with accepted communication theory. Also, studies have suggested that after listening to judicial instructions, jurors either do not understand the law of libel or ignore it when reaching a judgment.

A nonlegal researcher examining the problems of libel law may want to explore the communication questions inherent in the secondary rules contained in jury instructions. It is possible that the use or abuse of secondary rules in libel may have more to do with the "libel crisis" than the substantive First Amendment issues in libel law.

Judicial Review

From early 19th-century state court decisions such as *Respublica v. Passmore* (1802) to recent U.S. Supreme Court cases such as *Hustler Magazine v. Falwell* (1988), courts have played a major, if not the primary role, in defining the meaning of freedom of expression in the United States. Using the power of judicial review, state and federal courts hear challenges to government actions and establish the rules for the litigation of civil claims.[34]

Judicial review is a secondary rule central to the development of the law of freedom of expression. It is the "power of any court to hold unconstitutional and hence unenforceable any law, any official action based on law, or any other action by a public official that it deems . . . to be in conflict with the basic law, in the United States, its Constitution."[35]

The power of judicial review is not explicitly given to the judiciary by the Constitution. However, in *Marbury v. Madison* (1803) Chief Justice John Marshall asserted the power of the Supreme Court to measure government actions against the Constitution.[36] Marshall's claim of the power to review congressional and executive branch actions was controversial in 1803 and while today few challenge the legitimacy of judicial review, debate continues over the way in which courts should interpret the Constitution and the scope of the power of judicial review.

In Chapter 3, we will discuss the different legal theories used to interpret freedom of expression questions. Here it is important to be aware that the role of courts as the arbiters of disputes about the meaning of freedom of expression, which we take as a given in the late 20th century, is a judicially created mechanism. It is a secondary rule of law.

Advocacy and the Role of Litigants

The power of courts to use judicial review is limited by the passive role of courts in litigation. Courts are not in the business of offering unsolicited opinions about the law, and they are not able to reach out and bring litigants into a courtroom. A court may drop hints that it is interested in deciding a particular legal question, but must wait until a litigant brings a case before the bench before it is able to decide that particular point of law.

And even after a case is before a court, judges may address only those points of law raised by the litigants. These secondary rules constrain the power of judicial review, and they play an important role in shaping the development of legal doctrines.

One of the most famous and powerful First Amendment opinions in U.S. Supreme Court history, a concurring opinion written by Justice Louis Brandeis in *Whitney v. California* (1927), illustrates the importance of secondary rules. Anita Whitney was convicted under the Criminal Syndicalism Act of California for belonging to an organization that advocated criminal syndicalism, a doctrine that called for workers to seize control of the economy by direct means (as in a general strike). The Supreme Court upheld the conviction, finding that the law did not violate the due process clause of the 14th Amendment or the speech, press, or assembly clauses of the First Amendment.[37]

Justices Louis Brandeis and Oliver Wendell Holmes concurred in the result. Brandeis authored a stirring statement in support of freedom of expression:

> Those who won our independence believed that the final end of the state was to make men free to develop their facilities and that in its government the deliberative forces should prevail over the arbitrary. . . . They believed that freedom to think as you will and speak as you think are means indispensable to the discovery and spread of political truth. . . . Fear of serious injury cannot alone justify suppression of free speech and assembly. Men feared witches and burnt women. It is the function of speech to free men from the bondage of irrational fears.[38]

How could Brandeis write this strong First Amendment opinion and concur in the upholding of a conviction of a woman who had done little more than join and participate in meetings and conventions of the Communist Party of California?

Brandeis concurred because in the state trial and appellate courts Whitney's counsel had not framed the legal issues in a way that allowed the Supreme Court to reverse the state courts' rulings:

> Whether in 1919, when Miss Whitney did the things complained of, there was in California such clear and present danger of serious evil, *might have been the important issue in the case. She might have required that the issue be determined either by the court or the jury.* She claimed below that the statute as applied to her violated the Federal Constitution; but *she did not claim that it was void because there was no clear and present danger of serious evil, nor did she request that the existence of these conditions of a valid measure thus restricting the rights of free speech and assembly be passed on by the court or a jury. . . . [We] lack here the power . . . to correct in criminal cases vital errors* [italics added], although the objection was not taken in the trial court. Because we may not enquire into the errors now alleged, I concur in affirming the judgment of the state court.[39]

While Brandeis' opinion clearly indicates that he believed Whitney's First Amendment rights had been violated — that an examination of the facts would have demonstrated a definite lack of clear and present danger — the secondary rules which, generally stated, prohibit an appellate court from considering an appeal based on a legal claim not introduced at trial, tied his hands.

Given the voting breakdown in the case (seven of the nine justices joined the majority opinion), it is not likely that Brandeis could have attracted a majority to his view even if the clear and present danger claim had been raised. But the argument of Whitney's attorney precluded the possibility. The interpretation of clear and present danger advocated by Brandeis in 1927 did not attract a majority on the court until 1969, in the case of *Brandenburg v. Ohio*.[40]

Just as the failure to raise an issue will directly effect the outcome of a case, a poorly argued case can result in bad or unclear law. Courts must depend on the parties to a suit for the legal theories used to decide the case. While a court can direct counsel to address certain points of law, the court cannot ensure that the attorneys will do a good job.

Litigation is a forum for advocacy. Thus, the persuasive quality of the arguments presented on each side of the case will greatly influence the outcome of a case. When the legal principles at issue are not clearly delineated, the court's opinion or opinions may reflect the confusion or inadequacy of the legal arguments.

Arguably, First Amendment interests suffered in the Supreme Court's ruling in *Hazelwood v. Kuhlmeier* (1988), the high school press case that removed significant First Amendment protection for high school journalists, because the status of high school journalists and the role of school authorities as "publishers" were never clearly defined. The arguments before the court and the media commentary and editorial comment following the decision displayed the same division as found in the majority and dissenting opinions in the case.[41]

In some instances, secondary rules will determine litigation strategy, which in turn will determine whether a free press right exists. For example, in the state of Washington the State Supreme Court has developed a common law protection of confidential sources that under certain circumstances is more favorable to reporters than are the federal standards.[42] If a court orders a reporter to reveal a confidential source, the success of the legal strategy based on the reporter's right to keep sources confidential may turn on a question of jurisdiction. If the case can be argued as a matter of state law, the reporter stands a greater chance of success than if the case is argued as a question of federal law. Frequently, the ability to get a case into a favorable jurisdiction will determine whether the case is pursued.

While research in communication and law does not require that the communication researcher master the secondary rules of law, the researcher must appreciate the structure and process of law sufficiently to avoid errors of validity.

LEGAL CULTURE

The law is a social institution. Lawyers and judges are part of a specific professional culture which is bound in a particular time and place. Law can be viewed as reflecting the social values of the day, as a central influence on social values, or as both an influence and a reflector. The important point is that legal culture is embedded in the social culture of a given period in history. Understanding changes over time in the law of freedom of expression requires knowledge of the social values of the people practicing and using the law.

The Practice of Law

The relevance of the above theoretical concerns to the practice of law sometimes is hard to see. Legal practice is concerned with winning or avoiding legal disputes. Understanding legal theory is not the daily concern of practicing attorneys. They don't need to understand why the law exists in a certain way. Lawyers need to know how to use the law. Just as newspaper reporters and other media practitioners are fond of criticizing the academic focus of journalism and communication programs, practicing lawyers tend to dismiss "theory" as the irrelevant musing of academics in ivory towers. Of course, legal theory is implicit in the practice of law, just as communication theory is embedded in the practice of journalism, but when confronted with the question, "What is law," most legal practitioners would respond, "It's what I do every day."

The day in and day out practice of law for most lawyers is *not* arguing cases in trial or appellate courts. In fact, most lawyers rarely see the inside of a courtroom. They are involved in the process of keeping clients *out* of court. The legal theories and principles that appear in judge's opinions are less important than the question of what the law will allow a client to do or not do.

On a practical level, the lawyer is concerned with certainty, clarity, and predictability. When advising an advertiser that a particular claim in an ad is not deceptive under existing federal deceptive advertising regulation, the lawyer wants a clear set of rules upon which to base that advice. Questions of theoretical continuity have little immediate relevance to the lawyer's task.

Because of the concerns of legal practice, lawyers are trained to focus on particular cases, specific facts, and specific rules applicable to those facts. They are less concerned with generalizations or the ability to draw broad connections within the law. This pragmatic view of the practice of law is important to researchers examining freedom of the press. It represents an ignored influence on the law of freedom of expression.

Most academic writing about freedom of the press assumes that the development of free press law in the United States has been driven by libertarian theories of freedom of the press. Judicial opinion evokes a libertarian intent of the founding fathers and talks of the role of free expression in a democratic society. Media lawyers bolster legal claims with reference to the "watchdog" role of the press and the rights of individuals to express their personal beliefs. The rhetoric of freedom of the press asserts a causal link between libertarian theories and the law and constructs a logical progression from Blackstone to the 1980s. Only in recent years have historians, beginning with Leonard Levy in 1960, challenged that view.[43]

Certainly, liberal free press theory plays an important part in the development of free press law, but it is one of the arrows in the quiver of free press advocates, not the driving force in mass media litigation. Given a legal culture that is concerned with using the law to best serve the interests of clients regardless of the theoretical consistency of the argument made in any particular case, the researcher must take the pragmatic nature of legal practice into account when examining legal behavior and legal arguments.

For example, in the years since *New York Times v. Sullivan* (1964) the law of libel has been in a state of flux. When *Sullivan* was decided, most advocates of freedom of the press believed the case established strong protection for mass media in libel suits brought by public officials. While First Amendment theorists celebrated the court's decision to protect the "central meaning of the First Amendment" — the right to criticize government officials without fear of libel actions — the adoption, in 1964, of constitutional protection of libel cannot be explained by looking at only liberal free press theory.[44]

The decision must be viewed within the political context of the civil rights movement of the 1960s. The Supreme Court realized the need to stop southern politicians' use of libel laws against northern news organizations. The Court used the words of James Madison and the intent of the Founding Fathers as support for the decision, but the case was decided in response to political factors in 1964. There is no other way to explain the Court's discovery of a constitutional component of libel law 163 years after the adoption of the First Amendment.[45]

The strong protection established in *Sullivan* has not been realized in practice. Over the last 25 years libel law has been the major legal concern of mass media. Rather than creating a strong protection, many believe that libel law has had a "chilling effect" on mass media. Articles and reports calling for changes in the law of libel have become a staple in legal and journalism literature.[46]

But legal doctrine is only a part of the problem and may not be a major part of the *explanation* of the libel crisis. Several *social* factors add texture and richness to the picture.

We live in a litigious time. For many people in the United States, the law is the first resort when they have a complaint. Libel law may be a major problem for mass media because aggressive use of the law by public and private figures against media organizations is in agreement with social values of the day.

Rodney A. Smolla, in *Suing the Press* (1986), has suggested that a cultural embracing of libel as an acceptable way of responding to criticism in the media may partly explain the libel problem in the 1980s. Simply put, public persons, from Gen. William Westmoreland to the Rev. Jerry Falwell to Wayne Newton to former Miss America contestants and elected public officials brought libel suits because suing is an acceptable response to unfavorable stories in the press. While the number of libel suits filed appears to have peaked for the moment in the late 1980s, it is not clear that the downward trend is permanent. Smolla suggests that in a culture where self-improvement and physical appearance have become central to, if not obsessions of, the culture, acceptance of the use of libel as a means of protecting reputation is logical. While Smolla's theory is untested, it is provocative and illustrates the importance of viewing law as a social institution.[47]

The result of the threat of libel suits appears to be a "chilling effect." Media are less likely to publish or broadcast controversial stories because of the threat of being sued. Note that we didn't say fear of *losing* suits.

Studies show that libel law favors mass media. More than 90% of suits end in favor of media defendants, but changes in both legal rules and in accepted litigation practices make the cost of defending libel suits a major chilling factor.[48] The cost of litigation affects more than major media corporations. Small publications and citizen activists of all political persuasions claim to feel the chill of litigation costs. Libel law is part of the problem, but changes in accepted legal practice also contribute to the chill.

The practice of law has changed in the last 20 years. Changes in the rules of discovery allow lawyers greater freedom to gather evidence in the pretrial stages of litigation. Attorneys engage in aggressive, lengthy questioning of witnesses and parties to litigation before trial. As a result, a strategy of wearing an opponent down before trial has become accepted legal behavior. If a client can afford to pay for several years of pretrial filing of motions and years of deposition — the cost can run into the millions of dollars — an opportunity exists to win a case by harassing the opponent, rather than winning on the legal merits.

This use of litigation as a means of discouraging and wearing out an opponent — a "scorched earth" or "death march" strategy of litigation — is possible, in part, because of modern copying technology. It is now possible for voluminous records to be copied and transcripts to be printed at relatively low cost and in a matter of hours. As a result, the volume of documents in a fairly straightforward libel suit is now measured in pounds or feet rather than pages.

Production of documents and records costs money. The publisher of the *New York Times* and the editorial board of a local neighborhood association newsletter face the same question when deciding whether to publish criticism of an individual. Is publishing the information worth the costs of defending against a possible libel suit? The average cost for media defendants in libel litigation in 1986 exceeded $95,000.[49]

The practice of law is heavily influenced by questions of money. This is not inherently bad or wrong, but if we are to understand law within the context of legal culture, then we have to understand the effects of money on the practice of law. The ability of a client to pay for legal representation will affect the quality of counsel, the decision to take a case into court, the aggressiveness of the litigation, and the ability to appeal an adverse decision to a higher court.

Because litigation is expensive, free press rights are either not protected in practice in all situations or desired changes in the law are not achieved. In *Minnesota Rag* (1981), Fred Friendly tells the story of the litigation leading to *Near v. Minnesota* (1931), a landmark case in modern First Amendment case law. The name of Jay M. Near, the publisher of the *Saturday Press*, an anti-Semitic scandal sheet, would not have appeared in United States Reports were it not for Col. Robert McCormick, the publisher of the Chicago *Tribune*. McCormick supplied the money and the lawyers for Near's appeal of his conviction under Minnesota State law.[50]

Until the recent libel crisis, the first response of most if not all newspapers in the United States to a libel suit was to fight the case in court. Many publishers would publish material they believed to be true, and if sued, they would fight the suit in court. The conventional wisdom was that settling libel actions encouraged suits. Today, as a result of the litigation costs, lawyers frequently are consulted before potentially dangerous stories are published, and in some cases stories are not published because of the *possibility* of a libel suit. Rather than stand on a principle of always publishing truthful, accurate, newsworthy information, editors and publishers subject stories to a cost-benefit analysis. The question asked is whether the information is worth the cost of litigation.

The First Amendment rights of high school students provide another example. Gather together high school editors and reporters or contributors to school magazines, and they will recount numerous instances of violations of student press rights (even the minimal rights left after *Hazelwood*). Yet few of these cases are ever the subject of litigation. Unless the American Civil Liberties Union or another advocacy group funds a court challenge, students are unable to make use of existing constitutional protections. Parents are rarely willing or able to fund a court challenge costing thousands or even tens of thousands of dollars.

The importance of legal culture to the law of freedom of the press presents great opportunity to social research in law and communication. Once law is viewed as a social institution and not merely a set of formulas articulated by judges, the subject is opened for interdisciplinary and cross-disciplinary research. If the law is more than a collection of specialized rules accessible only to those trained in the law, then opportunities abound for informed research in communication and the law.

SCHOOLS OF LEGAL THOUGHT

Legal scholarship must be distinguished from the reams and reams of legal writing produced by legal practitioners. As used here, legal scholarship refers to writing concerned with understanding and explaining the law. While the brief written by an attorney or the opinion crafted by a judge are both examples of legal writing, they are examples of *doing* law. The judge or the attorney is using the law to achieve certain results. In contrast, a law review article or a legal treatise attempts to clarify and provide understanding of the law.

Shifts in legal scholarship in the 20th century have centered on changes in perceptions of the nature of judicial decision making and the relation of law to society. From the formalism or mechanical jurisprudence of the late 19th century to the Critical Legal Studies movement of the 1980s (these terms will be defined below), legal scholars have attempted to understand and explain the law by looking at the role of law in society and the role of judges in making, interpreting, or finding law.

Another way of talking about this question is to view it as a question about the "interplay of case and principle" in judicial decision making. In the 1980s the attack on "activist" judges, led by Edwin Meese, President Reagan's attorney general from 1980 to early 1988, under the banner of a "jurisprudence of original intent," has been an effort to turn judicial decision making toward a formalist conception of the proper role of judges. Judges, the "strict constructionists" would argue, should interpret, not make law.

Most legal scholars would argue that the popular understanding of this debate — that activist judges make law while strict constructionists are merely interpreting the text of existing laws or constitutions — does not reflect the understanding of the judicial function or law within mainstream legal scholarship. Adherents of competing schools of legal research may agree on little else, but they will agree that the question is far more complicated than the popular debate admits.[51]

While the discussion of these different schools of legal scholarship takes place in the rarefied atmosphere of law schools among law professors and a handful of judges and, to a lesser extent in other domains of the academic community, the influence of the debate spreads far beyond the halls of law schools as students exposed to the discussions enter legal practice or teaching, and as academics involved in the discourse are appointed to the bench or argue cases in court.

Each school of legal scholarship has influenced the practice of law and writing about law. The lines between the schools are frequently blurred. In practice, each new school influences the law, but the earlier traditions continue to exert an influence on legal thinking. As we enter the 1990s, legal scholars are challenging the dominant paradigms of legal scholarship. To understand the development of law in the United States in the 20th century, we must take into account this ferment in legal scholarship.

Formalism

Legal historian G. Edward White has described the dominant view of law in the 19th century: "Law was conceived of as a mystical body of permanent truths, and the judge was seen as one who declared what those truths were and made them intelligible — as an oracle who 'found' and interpreted the law." In the late 19th century this view of law as a fixed and rational body of existing truths was captured in a view of law as "legal science." Christopher Columbus Langdell became dean of Harvard Law School in 1870 and developed the case law method of studying law.

Langdell collected appellate cases, keeping those that agreed with established legal principles while discarding cases that did not fit into his formula. Students learned the law by reading appellate court decisions to discover the underlying legal principles. Law, as other "sciences," had an internal logic, consistent principles, and methods for determining the validity of a given legal theory.[52]

This method of deductive reasoning from "fundamental legal doctrines" became the dominant mode of legal scholarship in the late 19th century. As with other academic disciplines, legal scholarship focused on "ineluctable rules, principles, and axioms," and payed little attention to the outside world. It was a highly abstracted view of law. Logic, not result or effect, was the primary criterion for legal validity. In fact, the result of a legal principle was considered outside the control or domain of judges. The effect of the law on individuals and institutions was not part of the judicial decision-making equation.[53]

As many legal historians have demonstrated, the fundamental principles of legal science were not immutable neutral truths discovered in the science of law. The decisions of courts had effects on society, and frequently in the social turmoil of the late 19th and early 20th centuries the decisions of courts deduced from settled legal principle were in conflict with changing social conditions. Decisions such as *Plessy v. Ferguson* (1896), which established the separate but equal doctrine in equal protection cases, and *Lochner v. New York* (1905) that invalidated a state law limiting bakers to 10-hour workdays because it interfered with the bakers' property right to sell their services, were internally logical but ultimately out of touch with society.[54]

In the early 20th century, formalism came under concerted attack from both the bench and legal scholars. "Mechanical jurisprudence," as law professor Roscoe Pound called it in a 1908 *Columbia Law Review* article, did not recognize the relation of the law to society, nor did it accurately reflect the process of judicial decision making.[55]

Law was more than abstract arguments about internal logic. Oliver Wendell Holmes' biting dissent in *Lochner* challenged the central assumption of formalism: "The Fourteenth Amendment does not enact Mr. Herbert Spencer's Social Statics [sic]. . . .[A] Constitution is not intended to embody a particular economic theory, whether of paternalism and the organic relation of the citizen to the State or of laissez faire."[56]

If the law did not consist of unchanging fundamental principles, then formalism was not adequate to the task of understanding the law.

Sociological Jurisprudence

One reaction to formalism, or conceptualism as it is sometimes called, was a call for the use of social science evidence as part of the decision-making process. Courts needed to move away from reliance on universal principles and begin to recognize the relation of the law to contemporary American life.

The "Brandeis Brief," discussed in Chapter 4, is a landmark in the law. For the first time, the Supreme Court of the United States found studies of empirical phenomena relevant to the deciding of a legal question. The Court was careful to make clear that the harmful effects of long workdays were not a determining factor in its decision making; however the evidence did inform judicial interpretation of the constitutional language before the Court. The Oregon hours and wages law was constitutional because, notwithstanding the constitutional right of contract, the evidence showed that women needed to be protected from overly long working days as a matter of social policy.[57]

This use of social science as a means of scientific social policy making *and* judicial decision making added a new dimension to legal scholarship. Sociological jurisprudence did not replace formalism, but it breathed air into the vacuum of narrow, legalistic reasoning characteristic of formalist reasoning. Judges began to take notice of the effects of law and to consider evidence generated by social scientists. Advocates of sociological jurisprudence did not call for abandonment of legal principles and constitutional guarantees. Rather, to quote Roscoe Pound, it was a "movement for the adjustment of principles and doctrines to the human conditions they are to govern rather than to assumed first principles."[58] In other words, the law could not remain static in a changing world.

If judges had to evaluate the real world results of the law and were not confined to an abstract internally consistent set of legal principles, then the judicial decision-making process becomes a central concern. What do judges do? How do they reach decisions? What constrains the whims or biases of the judiciary?

Legal Realism

In 1930, Karl Llewellyn published "A Realistic Jurisprudence – The Next Step" in the *Columbia Law Review*. Llewellyn, responding to the growing influence of the behavioral and social sciences and sociological jurisprudence, called for a new focus in legal scholarship. He argued that the study of law should be the study of the *behavior* of judges and the relation of judicial behavior to legal rules. Instead of theorizing about whether the law should be based on assumptions of a rational, logical, consistent body of legal rules—the "paper rules"—Llewellyn and other legal Realists found the real rules of law to be impermanent, uncertain, inconsistent, and arbitrary. This dramatically different picture of the law could be explained by focusing on judicial behavior. Judges, the Realists observed, were not constrained by the paper rules. In every case before the bench, judges were confronted with choices between value alternatives. They made decisions based on personal value and belief systems and then constructed a legal argument to justify and rationalize the result.[59]

The Realists' relativistic, pragmatic view of the law as a problem-solving mechanism in which judges were not bound or for that matter guided by fixed moral or legal principles gained acceptance in the 1930s. However, as the United States turned its attention to the war in Europe in the late 1930s, moral relativism and law based on nothing more than the "realities" of modern society proved an uncomfortable position. The Realist movement did not die with the onset of World War II, but following the war legal scholars responded to the criticisms of the Realists by attempting to reconstruct a view of law based on something other than the sands of arbitrary judicial decision making.[60]

Reason Follows Realism

Beginning in the 1940s, legal scholars developed a view of law based on an assumption of rational, principled judicial decision making. Adherence to a neutral legal process based on bias-free principles, they argued, would prevent arbitrary decision making.

The rule of law and rational decision making have always been central assumptions of the Anglo-American legal system, but the Realists had challenged the assumptions. Now, scholars argued that rational decision making was more than an attribute of the legal system. It constrained the behavior of judges and would, if practiced, result in expression of consensually agreed upon social preferences.

The Realists exposed the human element of the law—judges were capable of arbitrary, biased behavior—now law professors such as Herbert Wechsler identified "neutral principles" and rationality as core values of the legal system. If judges were held to standards of rational, principled decision making, the rule of law, not arbitrary judicial behavior, would anchor the law.

Wechsler, in "Toward Neutral Principles of Constitutional Law," published in 1959, argued that principled decisions, that is, decisions "resting with respect to every step that is involved in reaching judgment on analysis and reasons quite transcending the immediate result that is achieved," distinguished the judicial process from the legislative and executive.[61]

Law professor Alexander Bickel, one of the most important advocates of analytical coherence and principled judicial decision making, expressed the perceived value of reasoned elaboration as a dominant decision-making paradigm in *The Supreme Court and the Idea of Progress* (1970):

> The insistence on reason in the judicial process in analytical coherence and on principled judgment no matter how narrow its compass, is traditional. Despite the countless lapses, it is an unmistakable thread in the fabric of our law — not alone the law of the Constitution — and of its literature. . . . The restraints of reason tend to ensure also the independence of the judge, to liberate him from the demands and fears — dogmatic, arbitrary, irrational, self- or group-centered — that so often enchain other public officials.[62]

Bickel argued that reliance on principle and reasoned elaboration insulated the judiciary from political pressures and from personal biases. If a judge was required to justify decisions using first principles, then consistency in the law would be preserved.[63]

Reasoned elaboration continues to be an important part of legal scholarship and teaching. Much energy is expended in law school classrooms in analysis of the stated and unstated principles found in judicial decisions. However, the belief that consensual values would be achieved as a result of reasoned elaboration did not survive unscathed the social turmoil of the civil rights movement, the Vietnam war, and the fragmenting of American society in the 1970s. The idea that consensus could be reached and would be reflected in the decisions of judges lost force as the divisions in our society became the focus of political discourse.

What remains is the requirement that judges give reasons for decisions and that the reasons transcend individual biases. A successful judicial opinion is one that effectively places the legal reasoning on sound legal principles and in the values that American society holds important. Such an opinion will meet societal standards of justice.

Law and Society

While some legal scholars in the 1950s focused on judicial decision making and reasoned elaboration, others took a broader view of the legal landscape. They viewed law as an instrumentality and attempted to explain legal phenomena in social terms. They wanted to understand how the law actually operates. This movement became known as the Law and Society movement. It is an interdisciplinary movement that uses the methods of social science and history to discover how law works and what it does.

While many scholars working in the Law and Society movement have policy views and objectives, the primary goal of the Law and Society studies is a better *understanding* of the law. This goal distinguishes the movement from sociological jurisprudence which uses social science evidence as part of a legal argument for a particular result in a legal conflict.

Legal history is one area where the Law and Society movement's influence has been great. In 1950, J. Willard Hurst, a law professor at the University of Wisconsin, published *The Growth of American Law*. It signaled a major change in legal history. "This was," law professor Robert Gordon wrote, "a history of law-making agencies — not only courts, but constitutional conventions, chief executives, administrative agencies, and the bar — inquiring into the social functions these agencies had served since the founding of the Republic." Hurst's "external legal history" dramatically changed the field of legal history and spawned a new form of legal history which attempts to place the law within the context of society and to identify the forces that influence the making of law. Instead of looking at judicial behavior or constraints on judicial decision making as the determinative forces in law, legal historians working in the Law and Society school look at social forces and the use of the law by individuals and institutions as determinative forces.[64]

Most of the current research in Law and Society uses social science method and theory to look at legal issues. In general, three questions are asked: (1) How is law created? (2) How does the law operate? (3) What is the impact of existing law?

Communication and law falls comfortably into the Law and Society school. As we have suggested throughout this discussion, one purpose of the study of communication and law is to create a means of examining communication phenomena in the law in order to understand better the relation of communication theory to the development of the law of freedom of the press.

In contrast to the other schools of legal research discussed, the Law and Society movement has a literature other than traditional law reviews. *Law and Society Review*, *Law & Social Inquiry*, and *Law and History Review* are three examples.

Critical Legal Studies

The Critical Legal Studies movement is a recent development in legal scholarship. The broad themes of the movement and much of its intellectual heritage are similar to that of critical movements in other fields. Here, the target is mainstream liberal legal thought. Since free press law in the United States is grounded in liberal political philosophy, the CLS movement offers a challenge and a potential for research.[65]

Liberalism is the dominant ideology in American law. All of the schools of legal scholarship discussed to this point accept liberalism and stop short of challenging it as a proper theoretical basis for a legal system. Members of the Critical Legal Studies movement, a young and diverse group of legal scholars, challenge the dominant liberal ideology. They borrow from a variety of disciplines — for example, philosophy, history, literary criticism — to fashion critiques that expose the inherent contradictions in liberal thought and to demonstrate the use of liberal theory to hide the contradictions.

CLS scholars have not paid a great deal of attention to free press issues, but a few authors have examined liberal concepts such as the "marketplace of ideas" and pointed out the contradictions between two aspects of liberal theory. The marketplace of ideas concept of free speech depends on the existence of a forum in which many voices are heard. Yet liberal theory also makes a distinction between public property and private property. Individuals have a right of access to public property (e.g., streets, parks) but little access to private property (e.g., newspapers, broadcast stations, cable systems).

CLS writers point out that the marketplace of ideas concept contains an inherent contradiction, especially if one looks at ownership patterns in the United States. And, they argue, the power of the marketplace of ideas as a legitimizing force is so strong that it gets in the way of finding a means to solve the problems of media access and participation in the United States.[66]

The long-term effect of the CLS movement on legal scholarship remains uncertain. However, the question is not whether the movement will have an effect, but rather the extent of its influence on legal scholarship.

Summary

We began this discussion of the law by identifying the importance of legal theory to an understanding of the law and by distinguishing the nature and use of theory in law and in scientific research. Legal theory is a normative theory used to established proper frameworks for ordering society.

Communication researchers entering the legal domain must be aware of the different uses of theory in the law and of the importance of legal rules on both legal results and communication behaviors in a legal setting. All cases which have First Amendment consequences are *not* decided on First Amendment grounds, and the law directs behavior in ways not found in other settings. Finally, the study of law has been influenced by a number of different schools of legal thought. In the 20th century, legal scholars have moved from a narrow focus on law as "legal science" to more complex interdisciplinary studies that view the law as part of a larger social context.

NOTES

1. Morton J. Horwitz, *The Transformation of American Law* (Cambridge, Mass., 1977): xi.

2. Donna A. Demac, *Liberty Denied* (New York, 1988): 101.

3. United States v. Snepp, 456 F.Supp. 176 (E.D.Va. 1978).

4. 595 F.2d 926 (4th Cir. 1979).

5. 444 U.S. 507 (1980).

6. New York Times v. Sullivan, 376 U.S. 254, 280 (1964).

7. St. Amant v. Thompson, 390 U.S. 727, 731 (1968).

8. Brueggemeyer v. ABC, 684 F.Supp. 452 (N. Tex. 1988).

9. Abraham Kaplan, *The Conduct of Inquiry* (New York, 1964): 302.

10. William Read, *Legal Thinking* (Philadelphia, 1986): 184.

11. John Finch, *Introduction to Legal Theory* (London, 1974): 1.

12. Ibid., 18.

13. John Finnis, "Comment," in Ruth Gavison, ed., *Issues in Contemporary Legal Philosophy* (New York, 1987): 70.

14. Philip Soper, "Choosing Legal Theory on Moral Grounds," in Jules Coleman and Ellen Paul, eds., *Philosophy and Law* (New York, 1987): 33.

15. H.L.A. Hart, *The Concept of Law* (Oxford, 1961): B.

16. Lee C. Bollinger, *The Tolerant Society* (New York, 1986): 72.

17. Aviam Soifer, "Freedom of the Press in the United States," in Pnina Lahav, ed., *Press Law in Modern Democracies* (New York, 1985): 79.

18. Karl Llewellyn, "The Problem of Defining Law," *Columbia Law Review* 30 (1930): 431.

19. Lon L. Fuller, *The Morality of Law* (New Haven, 1969): 106; Wallace D. Loh, *Social Research in the Judicial Process* (New York, 1984): 637.

20. Henry J. Abraham, *The Judicial Process*, 5th ed. (New York, 1986): 7; Michael Martin, *The Legal Philosophy of H.L.A. Hart* (Philadelphia, 1987): 176.

21. Hart, *Concept of Law*, 182.

22. Ruth Gavison, "Comment," 29.

23. Charles Evans Hughes, 1907 speech quoted in William B. Lockhart, Yale Kamisar, and Jesse H. Choper, *Constitutional Rights and Liberties*, 5th ed. (St. Paul, Minn., 1980): 8.

24. Ronald Dworkin, *Taking Rights Seriously* (Cambridge, Mass., 1977): 184.

25. Laurence H. Tribe, *Constitutional Choices* (Cambridge, Mass., 1985): 188.

26. John Roche, "Civil Liberty in the Age of Enterprise," *University of Chicago Law Review* 31 (1963): 103.

27. Near v. Minnesota, 283 U.S. 697 (1931).

28. Red Lion Broadcasting v. FCC, 395 U.S. 367, 390 (1969).

29. Miami Herald Publishing Co. v. Tornillo, 418 U.S. 241, 258 (1974).

30. See, for example, Lee C. Bollinger, "Freedom of the Press and Public Access," *Michigan Law Review* 75 (1976): 1; Patrick Parsons, *Cable Television and the First Amendment* (Lexington, Mass., 1987).

31. Lawrence M. Friedman, *A History of American Law*, 2nd ed. (New York, 1988): 17.

32. Hruby v. Kalina, 424 N.W.2d 130 (Neb. 1988).

33. Hart, *The Concept of Law*, 92.

34. Respublica v. Passmore 3 Yeats 440 (Pa. 1802); Hustler Magazine v. Falwell 108 S.Ct. 876 (1988).

35. Abraham, *Judicial Process*, 192.

36. Marbury v. Madison, 1 Cranch 137 (1803).

37. Whitney v. California, 274 U.S. 357, 375–77 (1927).

38. Ibid., 375–377.

39. Ibid., 379.

40. Brandenberg v. Ohio, 395 U.S. 444 (1969).

41. Hazelwood School District v. Kuhlmeier, 108 S.Ct. 562 (1988). See, for example, *Press Review*, Indiana High School Press Assn. (March-April 1988); "Limit on Student Speech," editorial, *The Des Moines Register* (25 January 1988): 3A; "Open Season on the High School Press," *Columbia Journalism Review* (March-April 1988): 18.

42. State v. Rinaldo, 684 P.2d 392 (Wa. 1984); Clampitt v. Thurston County, 658 P.2d 641 (Wa. 1983); Senear v. Daily Journal-American, 641 p.2d 1180 (Wa. 1982).

43. Wm. David Sloan and Thomas Schwartz, "Freedom of the Press, 1690–1801," *American Journalism* 5 (1988): 159; Timothy W. Gleason," Historians and Freedom of the Press Since 1800," *American Journalism* 5 (1988): 230.

44. Harry Kalven, Jr., "The New York Times Case," *The Supreme Court Review* (1964): 192.

45. Samuel Pierce, "The Anatomy of an Historic Decision," *North Carolina Law Review* 43 (1965): 315; Anthony Lewis, "*New York Times v. Sullivan* Reconsidered," *Columbia Law Review* 83 (1983): 603.

46. For example, Judy D. Lynch, "Public Officials, the Press, and the Libel Remedy," *Oregon Law Review* 67 (1988): 611; Annenberg Washington Program, *Proposal for the Reform of Libel Law* (Washington, D.C., 1988); Gannett Center for Media Studies, *The Cost of Libel* (New York, 1986); "Rewriting Libel Law," *The American Lawyer* (July-August 1986): 6.

47. Rodney A. Smolla, *Suing the Press* (New York, 1986); see also David Reisman, "Democracy and Defamation," *Columbia Law Review* 42 (1942): 730; Timothy W. Gleason, " 'Our Abominable Libel Laws,' " paper delivered to West Coast Journalism Historians Conference (1989).

48. Randall P. Bezanson, Gilbert Cranberg, and John Soloski, *Libel Law and the Press* (New York, 1987); Marc A. Franklin, "Winners and Losers and Why," *American Bar Foundation Research Journal* (1980): 455; "Suing the Media for Libel," *American Bar Foundation Research Journal* (1981): 797.

49. Bezanson, *Libel Law and the Press*, 293, ftn. 36.

50. Near v. Minnesota, 283 U.S. 697 (1931); Fred W. Friendly, *Minnesota Rag* (New York, 1981).

51. G. Edward White, *Tort Law in America* (New York, 1985): 110. For contrasting views on constitutional interpretation see Laurence H. Tribe, *Constitutional Choices* (Cambridge, Mass., 1985); Christopher Wolfe, *The Rise of Modern Judicial Review* (New York, 1986); see also Loh, *Social Research*, 637–694.

52. G. Edward White, *The American Judicial Tradition* (New York, 1976): 2. For discussions of Langdell's influence in legal scholarship and education see Grant Gilmore, *The Ages of American Law* (New Haven, 1977); Robert Stevens, *Law School* (Chapel Hill, 1983); Lawrence M. Friedman, *A History of American Law*, 2nd ed. (New York, 1988).

53. G. Edward White, "From Sociological Jurisprudence to Realism: Jurisprudence and Social Change in Early Twentieth-Century America," *Virginia Law Review* 58 (1972): 1001; Loh, *Social Research, 658.*

54. Plessy v. Ferguson, 163 U.S. 537 (1896); Lochner v. New York, 198 U.S. 45 (1905).

55. Roscoe Pound, "Mechanical Jurisprudence," *Columbia Law Review* 8 (1908): 605.

56. Lochner v. New York, 198 U.S. 45, 75 (1905).

57. Muller v. Oregon, 208 U.S. 412 (1908).

58. Quoted in White, "From Sociological Jurisprudence to Realism," 1004.

59. Karl Llewellyn, "A Realistic Jurisprudence — The Next Step," *Columbia Law Review* 30 (1930).

60. G. Edward White, *Tort Law in America* (New York, 1980): 140–6.

61. Herbert Wechsler, "Toward Neutral Principles of Constitutional Law," *Harvard Law Review* (1959): 15.

62. Alexander Bickel, *The Supreme Court and the Idea of Progress* (New Haven, 1970): 81–82.

63. Ibid; G. Edward White, "The Evolution of Reasoned Elaboration," *Virginia Law Review* 59 (1973): 279; Loh, *Social Research*, 676–678.

64. J. Willard Hurst, *The Growth of American Law* (Boston, 1950); Robert W. Gordon, "J. Willard Hurst and the Common Law Tradition in American Legal History," *Law and Society Review* 10 (1975): 9.

65. For an introduction to Critical Legal Studies see Roberto M. Unger, *The Critical Legal Studies Movement* (Cambridge, Mass., 1986); Mark Kelman, *A Guide to Critical Legal Studies* (Cambridge, Mass., 1987).

66. See, for example, Stanley Ingber, "The Marketplace of Ideas," *Duke Law Journal* (1984): 1; David Kairys, "Freedom of Speech," and Mark Tushnet, "Corporations and Free Speech," in Kairys, ed., *The Politics of Law* (New York, 1982): 140, 253.

3

THEORIES OF FREEDOM OF EXPRESSION

The concept of freedom of expression presents difficult problems of interpretation and understanding. The texts of federal and state constitutional speech and press clauses are not self-defining. Students of free expression continue to seek theories that will lead to better understanding of the meaning of freedom of expression.

A variety of approaches has been developed for thinking about freedom of expression. For the most part, those who turn their attention to this task are attempting to provide a rationale for strengthening or broadening legal protection for expression. However, some theorists are at least equally concerned with *understanding*. Harry Kalven best expressed the importance of understanding freedom of expression:

> If my puzzle as to the First Amendment is not a true puzzle, it can only be for the congenial reason that free speech is so close to the heart of democratic organization that if we do not have an appropriate theory for our law here, we feel we really do not understand the society in which we live.[1]

In every case, the theorist's task is to develop criteria for interpreting and understanding the meaning of the First Amendment to the Constitution of the United States or state constitutional freedom of speech and press clauses.

The concept of freedom of the press presents difficult problems of interpretation and understanding. Because freedom of expression guarantees found in the law are not self-defining, a good theory of freedom of expression should provide a framework for thinking about and defining freedom of expression within a given cultural or political context. As the Ayatollah Ruholla Khomeini's call for the death of author Salman Rushdie because of his book, *The Satanic Verses*, and the subsequent controversy in the Islam and western worlds demonstrated, the meaning of "freedom of the press" is bound by political and cultural contexts.[2]

Protections of freedom of the press found in the First Amendment and in state constitutions are broadly worded texts with little definitional value. The First Amendment says, "Congress shall make no law abridging . . . freedom of speech, or of the press." Only two states, Hawaii and South Carolina, have constitutional free press clauses with language that parallels the First Amendment.

Thirty-nine state constitutions have free press provisions which qualify the right with a statement of responsibility. For example, Article 1, Section 8 of the Oregon Constitution reads, "No law shall be passed restraining the free expression of opinion or restricting the right to speak, write or print freely on any subject whatsoever: But every person shall be responsible for the abuse of this right."

The federal and state constitutions establish rights to freedom of expression, but the texts do not define the limits of constitutional protection. The general thrust of both the First Amendment and state constitutional speech and press clauses are similar, but some state supreme courts have interpreted state clauses as providing more protection for expression.[3]

The Oregon Supreme Court has been one of the leaders in the use of the state constitution. The question of constitutional protection of obscene speech in Oregon provides one of the starkest examples of the indeterminacy of constitutional texts.

Under the First Amendment to the Constitution of the United States, sexually explicit speech loses First Amendment protection if the government is able to show the trier of fact (a jury or judge) that the speech meets the legal definition of obscenity established in the case of *Miller v. California* (1973). Under *Miller*, the government must show that the expression in question meets the following standard:

(1) An average person, applying contemporary local standards, finds that the work taken as a whole appeals to a prurient interest.

(2) The work depicts in a patently offensive way sexual conduct specifically defined by applicable state law.

(3) The work lacks serious literary, artistic, political, or social value as defined by a reasonable person.[4]

Chief Justice Warren Burger writing for the majority said that the government has a proper role to play in defining and controlling the distribution of sexually explicit speech:

The protection given speech and press was fashioned to assure unfettered interchange of *ideas* for the bringing about of political and social changes desired

> by the people. . . . We do not see the harsh hand of censorship of ideas — good or bad, sound or unsound — and repression of political liberty lurking in every regulation of commercial exploitation of human interest in sex.[5]

Certain speech, the Chief Justice reasoned, does not contribute to the intellectual discourse of the society, and therefore the government can ban that speech.

In *State v. Henry* (1986), however, the Oregon Supreme Court interpreted the state constitutional protection of the right to speak, write, or print freely on any subject *whatsoever* to prohibit the state from *defining* unprotected categories of expression. In other words, the state court said the *Miller* test violated the state constitution.

The two cases can be explained using a textual analysis — the language of Article 1, Section 8 is broader than the language of the First Amendment — but dicta in Justice J.J. Jone's majority opinion in *Henry* is more enlightening:

> The problem with the United State Supreme Court's approach to obscene expression is that it permits government to decide what constitutes socially acceptable expression which is precisely what Madison decried: "The difficulty (with the United State Supreme Court's approach) arises from the anomaly that the very purpose of the First Amendment is to protect expression which fails to conform to community standards."[6]

The Oregon Supreme Court rejected Justice Burger's claim that government has a proper role to play in defining the value of categories of expression.

How can the researcher make sense of these two contradictory opinions, or sort out the merits of the dissenting opinions filed in the cases? To do more than agree or disagree with the conclusions reached, we must identify and examine the free expression theories that shaped the justices' interpretations of constitutional free expression clauses.

The modern development of free expression theory is a surprisingly recent enterprise in the law, and to date, while the literature is impressive, few serious students would suggest that we have developed a satisfactory theoretical framework for discussing freedom of expression.[7] As a result, much of the discussion is muddied by competing assertions of values and interests based on different theories of freedom of expression. Frequently, the theoretical disagreements are submerged in a sea of rhetorical flourish. Law professor Lee C. Bollinger recently observed that "the official language of the First Amendment derives . . . from the enlightenment era, and so we frequently encounter heavy doses of talk about tyrannical tendencies of governments and the rationality of people."[8]

Clearly, the free press issues of the late 20th century cannot be understood in that framework. A more complex means of analysis is required. This chapter introduces various theories of freedom of expression to enable sorting out what people *mean* from what they *say* when talking about freedom of expression.

A cautionary note: We are talking about free expression theories in this chapter, and that focus will limit the discussion. It is dangerous to assume that a judge's view of freedom of speech and press will always be determinative in "free press cases" or that a strong correlation always exists between a judge's view of freedom of the press and a conservative or liberal jurisprudence. In some cases, such as the *Snepp* case discussed in Chapter 2, the case pivots on other legal issues, and in other cases, for example *Hustler Magazine v. Falwell* (1988) — a libel and intentional infliction of emotional distress case raising First Amendment questions — a "conservative" justice will write a "liberal" First Amendment opinion.[9]

THE MARKETPLACE OF IDEAS

In *Abrams v. United States* (1919), Justice Oliver Wendell Holmes writing in dissent introduced the metaphor at the heart of 20th-century liberal free press theory. Echoing the free press ideas first suggested by John Milton in the 17th century, central to the free speech thinking of English and American revolutionaries in the 18th century and expanded upon by John Stuart Mill in the 19th century, Holmes wrote:

> But when men have realized that time has upset many fighting faiths, they may come to believe even more than they believe the very foundations of their own conduct that the ultimate good desired is better reached by free trade in ideas — that the best test of truth is the power of thought to get itself accepted in the competition of the marketplace, and that truth is the only ground upon which their wishes safely can be carried out. That at any rate is the theory of our Constitution. It is an experiment, as all life is an experiment.[10]

The marketplace metaphor captures the central themes of free press theory in the United States: (1) The pursuit of truth is best accomplished when the people are exposed to competing ideas; (2) In order for the marketplace to function, the government must play a minimal role in the trade of ideas; (3) The clash of ideas *will* result in the discovery of "truth";

(4) The existence of a functioning marketplace of ideas serves the interests of individuals in the society and the good of the society.

While the marketplace metaphor is open to challenge — we will discuss some of its critics below — it has framed free press theorizing in the 20th century. The question asked by most authors is not, should the marketplace exist, but rather, how should the marketplace be defined and regulated?

The brief discussion of each one of the myriad approaches is intended to provide a general idea of the approach and to encourage you to explore all or at least several of the theories. In some cases the theories overlap, and in others we seem to be comparing apples, oranges, and kumquats. Indeed, that is the problem. The list is not inclusive, but it will give you a sense of the literature.

JUDICIAL DOCTRINES

Constitutional guarantees of freedom of expression are not self-defining. (In legal language, the "text is not determinative.") When courts are confronted with the problem of defining constitutional protection in a specific case, the judge or judges must choose a legal strategy to decide the case. The strategy will be determined by the judges' views of the law and the role of courts (the jurisprudence of the court), and the legal issues raised in the case before the court.

In First Amendment cases, judges have developed several different jurisprudential strategies. They reflect important elements of free expression theory, understanding of the history of free expression, and the place of free expression in the constitutional framework.

Original Intent

Original intent is a theory of jurisprudence often used in support of liberal interpretations of freedom of expression. Under the "doctrine of original intent," as it is frequently called, the determinative factor in interpreting the First Amendment should be the intent of the "framers" of the Bill of Rights. When judges attempt to discover the meaning of the speech and press clauses of the First Amendment, they should ascertain the intent of the framers and limit interpretation to that discovered intent.

While this doctrine is not a First Amendment theory in a strict sense, it is so intertwined with a liberal theory of freedom of the press that it can be considered a free expression theory. Advocates of original intent theory begin with an assumption that the drafters of the First Amendment and the other amendments that comprise the Bill of Rights intended to create broad protection for freedom of speech and the press.

Some scholars explain this liberal framers' intent in terms of a natural right theory, which holds that the framers believed that government could not suppress speech because the right to speak was inalienable. Others, for example Professor Vincent Blasi who developed a "checking theory" of framers' intent, argue that the First Amendment was a means to the end of democratic government. Blasi theorized that the First Amendment was drafted in order to create a check on the abuse of government power. This view is also seen in scholarship which finds an intent to create a special protection for "the press" in the press clause.[11]

The assumption that the framers had a liberal intent as we understand that phrase in the 20th century is widely held and has been a centerpiece of First Amendment thinking for most of the 20th century, but it rests on less-than-certain historical evidence.

Writers, such as law professor David Anderson and journalism historian Jeffery A. Smith, have used historical analysis to attempt to ascertain to the limited extent possible the meaning of freedom of the press in 1791, the year the First Amendment was ratified. However, intent is a difficult historical question, and the evidence in support of a "liberal" intent in 1791 is, at best, inconclusive. It is clear that the press in the late 1700s was vibrant and caustic, but it is far less clear that the framers intended the First Amendment as a bar to government regulation of the press.

Until 1960, the assumption of a liberal original intent stood unchallenged in the 20th century. However, in 1960, historian Leonard Levy's *Legacy of Suppression*, a history of the First Amendment, raised serious doubt about liberal original intent theory. Levy's revisionist history determined that

> the generation that framed the first state declarations of rights and the First Amendment was hardly as libertarian as we have traditionally assumed. . . . A broad libertarian theory of freedom of speech and press did not emerge in the United States until the Jeffersonians, then a minority party, were forced to defend themselves against the Federalist Sedition Act of 1798.[12]

Levy based his conclusion on an historical analysis of the law and theory of freedom of the press in the late 1700s.

Smith, whose book *Printers and Press Freedoms* is the most ambitious attempt to refute Levy, focused on the practice of freedom of the press in the same period. Anderson looked at the language of free press clauses in state constitutions prior to the drafting of the First Amendment.[13]

The result of the historical analysis of the intent of the framers of the First Amendment is uncertainty. Professors Wm. David Sloan and Thomas Schwartz have concluded that "out of the debate will emerge a view of early American attitudes that takes a middle ground between libertarianism, both the traditional and new versions, and Levy's viewpoint."[14] While this may satisfy the historian, it only confuses the legal analysis and erodes the power of original intent theories of freedom of the press. If the intent is not clear, then it cannot be the determinative factor in constitutional interpretation of freedom of the press.

The uncertainty of the historical evidence of original intent does not mean that judges are free to pour whatever meaning they wish into the text of the speech and press clauses of the First Amendment. They are still bound to the task of interpreting the meaning of a constitutional protection. Thus, the efforts of First Amendment scholars have been to determine the proper criteria for interpreting, "Congress shall make no law . . . abridging the freedom of speech, or of the press."

Clear and Present Danger

When Holmes first used the clear and present danger test in *Schenck v. the United States* (1919), he limited government authority to suppress speech advocating unlawful conduct to circumstances where it could show that the speech was a "clear and present danger" to the public welfare. Speech could be regulated if "the words are used in such circumstances and are of such a nature as to create a clear and present danger that they will bring about the substantive evils that Congress has the right to prevent."[15]

Holmes' clear and present danger test prompted law professor Zechariah Chafee, Jr. to write *Freedom of Speech* (1920), the seminal 20th-century defense of the marketplace of ideas and of clear and present danger. Chafee called clear and present danger "a test of great value for determining the true scope of the First Amendment" and said it was the first "authoritative judicial interpretation in accord with the purpose of the framers of the Constitution."[16]

However, the test provided little protection for expression prior to the 1940s. In *Schenck* and a number of subsequent cases, the Court noted the clear and present test and either found the expression violated the test or did not use it to decide the case.

The "clear and present danger" test continues to be an important line-drawing tool in First Amendment jurisprudence, even though it has been widely criticized and has been interpreted and reinterpreted by the courts over the past 70 years. Advocates of clear and present danger argue that it is the best available judicial test for striking a proper balance between protection of the marketplace of ideas and the need to protect the national security and the public order. Opponents argue that history shows the test to be open to widely varying interpretations and to have provided little or no protection to radical speech in times of political stress.[17]

Dissatisfaction with the clear and present danger test as a protection for radical speech and the need for First Amendment standards to deal with other types of free expression questions require a variety of alternative judicial strategies in free expression law.

(Nearly) Absolutist

Supreme Court Justices Hugo Black and William O. Douglas believed that the "no law" language in the First Amendment meant *no* law. They argued that the First Amendment provided unconditional protection of expression. However, even the absolutists stopped short of interpreting the First Amendment as an absolute ban on *all* governmental authority to control expression.[18]

Justice Douglas was a fervent advocate of absolute protection of freedom of speech and press. In his 36 years on the Court, he consistently articulated (frequently in dissent) a vision of the First Amendment as a nearly insurmountable barrier to government interference with the peoples' right to freedom of the press.

Douglas believed that the marketplace of ideas was central to democracy and that only in extreme situations could the government enter the marketplace. In *Dennis v. United States* (1951), in dissent, he wrote:

> There comes a time when even speech loses its constitutional immunity. . . . When conditions are so critical that there will be no time to avoid the evil that the speech threatens, it is time to call a halt. . . . Yet free speech is the rule, not the exception. . . . There must be some immediate injury to society that is likely if speech is allowed.[19]

Over the years, Douglas found few situations where conditions warranted government action against speech. He argued that the First Amendment barred regulation of obscenity, punishment of libels, permit and license regulations, and breach of the peace statutes where speech constituted the basis for regulation, and he argued for protection of symbolic expression.

Douglas' absolutistism was grounded in a faith in the validity of the marketplace of ideas. Speech was central to the democratic process and he believed debate fueled democracy:

> The vitality of civil and political institutions in our society depends on free discussion. . . . Accordingly a function of free speech under our system of government is to invite dispute. It may indeed best serve its high purpose when it induces a condition of unrest, creates dissatisfaction with conditions as they are, or even stirs people to anger.[20]

Because he believed that freedom of expression required the taking of risks and stopping expression only when it created an imminent danger to society, Douglas used a very narrow reading of the clear and present danger test to draw a line between protected and unprotected speech.

In a 1960 lecture, Black said, "It is my belief that there *are* 'absolutes' in our Bill of Rights, and that they were put there on purpose by men who knew what words meant and meant their prohibitions to be 'absolutes.' " If the First Amendment "means what it says," Black said, then the Constitution prohibited any federal abridgment of speech or press.[21]

However, Black's absolutism was limited by a narrow reading of the forms of expression that constituted speech. His speech/action distinction allowed him to find some expression — for example, picketing, symbolic structures, and sit-ins — to be action rather than speech and therefore beyond the absolute protection of the First Amendment speech and press clauses. The limits of the speech-action distinction are seen in *Cohen v. California* (1971).

Paul Robert Cohen walked down a corridor in the Los Angeles County Courthouse in 1968 wearing a jacket with the words, "Fuck the Draft" displayed on the back. He was arrested for "offensive conduct" which a California court defined as "*behavior* which has a tendency to provoke *others* to acts of violence or to in turn disturb the peace." In other words, Cohen was not arrested for *communicating* a political message, but rather for *displaying* the message in an inappropriate manner in that particular forum.

The U.S. Supreme Court overturned Cohen's conviction: "The conviction quite clearly rests upon the asserted offensiveness of the *words* Cohen used to convey the message to the public. The only 'conduct' which the State sought to punish is the fact of communication." Since the state can in all but special circumstances regulate only the time, place, and manner of expression, the conviction violated the First Amendment.[22]

But Black joined Justices Blackmun and Burger in dissent. They argued that "Cohen's absurd and immature antic . . . was mainly conduct and little speech." Therefore, the action could be punished by the state.[23]

Communication students will find legal efforts to determine a bright or even a faintly glowing line between "expression" and "conduct" to border on the absurd. The idea that conduct is not expressive is not valid from a communication perspective, but it points out the task confronting free expression theorists. Freedom of expression is not an absolute; thus, as communication professor Franklyn Haiman writes in *Speech and Law in a Free Society* (1981),

> The right to freedom of speech sometimes must give way to competing concerns. But it should not give way simply because acts, rather than words, were the vehicle for expression. If justifications are to be found for restraining communicative behavior they must be found in the context and in the effects of that communication upon other fundamental interests.[24]

BALANCING THEORIES

. Constitutional protection of freedom of the press at either the state or federal level requires the weighing of competing constitutional interests. For example, the Federal Constitution protects both freedom of speech and the right of property owners to control the use of private property. Balancing is a strategy for addressing conflicting constitutional interests in a specific case.

So, assume an antinuclear advocate wishes to make a speech against the use of nuclear power at a shopping center several miles from a nuclear power plant construction site because most of the residents of the community shop there rather than in the downtown shopping area. However, the owner of the shopping center refuses to allow the speech. In fact, the owner has the speaker arrested for trespassing. At trial, the speaker claims a First Amendment right to speak at the shopping center. The owner of the shopping center claims the speaker trespassed on private property. And, he states that he supports nuclear power.

How should the court sort out these competing claims? Which one should be given preference, the right to speak or the right to control the use of private property?[25]

Ad Hoc Balancing

If the court uses an ad hoc balancing theory, it begins with the assumption that all rights in the Constitution are of equal weight, and governmental actions are presumed to be in agreement with the Constitution. All rights and all governmental actions will be treated as equal when a right is used to challenge government action or competing rights in litigation. The facts of each case will decide the outcome on a case-by-case basis.

In one case the facts may favor speech rights and in another property rights. This is not to suggest that courts will be arbitrary in deciding the case. Rather, it means that the conflicting rights at issue are viewed as equal under the Constitution and will be given equal weight in analyzing the case. The decision will be based on a weighing of the factual issues presented to the court.

To return to the antinuclear speaker arrested for trespassing, a court using an ad hoc balancing strategy might weigh the importance of the speaker's message against the degree to which the speaker infringed the shopping center owner's use of the property. A court might decide that under some circumstances the First Amendment does create a right of access to private property. If the speaker's message is important to public debate and the speech does not significantly affect the operation of the shopping center, then the speaker should have the right to reach the audience at the shopping center. However, had the speaker created a significant disturbance, the court might find that the property owner's rights had been infringed.

Or the court might find that because the right to speak is no more important in the constitutional scheme than the right to property, it does not create any right to use private property against the owner's wishes; therefore, the trespassing conviction is proper.

Preferred Position Balancing

Under a preferred position theory, some rights are viewed as being "preferred freedoms." In *United States v. Carolene Products* (1938), a federal economic regulation case, Justice Harlan F. Stone suggested in a footnote that the explicitly stated rights found in the Bill of Rights required more protection under the Constitution. In cases where governmental action is challenged as violating Bill of Rights protections, courts are required to place the individual right in a preferred position:

There may be a narrower scope for operation of the presumption of constitutionality when legislation appears on its face to be within a specific prohibition of the Constitution, such as those of the first ten amendments, which are deemed equally specific when held to be embraced within the Fourteenth. . . .

It is unnecessary to consider now whether legislation which restricts those political processes which can ordinarily be expected to bring about the repeal of undesirable legislation, is to be subjected to more exacting scrutiny under the general prohibitions of the Fourteenth Amendment than are most other types of legislation.[26]

In practice, the value to freedom of expression of its status as a preferred freedom is that the government carries a heavy burden whenever a governmental action is challenged as a violation of free expression protection. In cases such as *New York Times v. United States* and *United States v. Washington Post* (1971), the Pentagon Papers cases, press interests were victorious because the government was unable to meet the burden of proof required to overcome the preferred position given the First Amendment.[27]

Use of the phrase "preferred position" is less common today than it was 20 years ago, but the principle remains. Judges using a preferred position theory are balancing free expression interests against other interests, but they are balancing with a thumb on the First Amendment side of the scale. It may not be enough to tilt the scale to the First Amendment side in every case, but it favors free expression interests.

CATEGORICAL APPROACHES

All expression is not treated the same way under the First Amendment. In First Amendment jurisprudence *political* speech enjoys the broadest First Amendment protection. In general terms, political speech is truthful speech or statements of opinion concerning government, or expression that contributes to the governing process. In practice, political expression is more easily defined in negative terms — it is speech that does not fall into a less-protected category of expression.

Certain kinds of speech are considered to be outside of First Amendment protection and other types of speech are given less constitutional protection. Each category is treated differently. All but one of the categories are content-based distinctions: that is, the content of the expression determined the category of speech. Broadcast speech, a technological-based distinction, is the only First Amendment category that is not content-based.

Libel and Privacy

Libelous speech and speech that invades a person's privacy are two of the most important categories of expression that fall outside of First Amendment protection. Both libel and privacy law developed as torts in the common law and only recently became questions of constitutional law.

A tort is a legal wrong done to another person. In order for a tort to occur, a person must have a legal duty to another person; the duty must be breached; and a harm must result.

Under common law libel, speakers have a duty to make truthful statements about the reputations of others. If a false, defamatory statement is made, the speaker's duty to the defamed person is breached and the law presumes reputational harm. The history of the tort of libel begins in early English law. There is some dispute over the status of the crime of seditious libel under the First Amendment in 1791, but in practice, courts did not view libel as a First Amendment question until 1964. In *New York Times v. Sullivan* (1964), the United States Supreme Court held that the common law standards did not create adequate protection for public debate on matters of public interest.[28]

The tort of privacy is quite young when compared to libel. Protection for individuals from the publication of "private facts" or from the use of their names or likenesses to sell products or services began to develop in the late 19th century.[29]

In the 20th century the tort has been divided into four distinct parts: publication of private facts, wrongful appropriation of a person's name or likeness for commercial purposes, the physical invasion of an individual's privacy, and false light invasion of privacy. The four areas of privacy are concerned with the concept of privacy in a very general sense, but each deals with a distinct (and not necessarily consistent) notion of privacy. In the areas of false light privacy and publication of private facts, the First Amendment has influenced the common law, but to a great extent privacy law remains a common law tort.

Within libel and privacy law, a balance has been struck between the interests of individual reputation, the individual's right to privacy and control of one's name or likeness, and freedom of expression. The balance is not permanently fixed and in cases such as *New York Times v. Sullivan* and *Time, Inc. v. Hill* (1967) the Supreme Court has adjusted it, but the basic premise that certain speech falls outside of First Amendment protection because it is libelous or an invasion of privacy remains.[30]

Obscenity

Obscenity is a category of expression that has *no* protection under the First Amendment, but is at the same time, the hardest to define. Justice Potter Stewart summed up the problem in *Jacobellis v. Ohio* (1964) when he admitted difficulty in defining obscene speech, but said, "I know it when I see it."[31]

The legal distinction between obscene material and pornographic or sexually explicit material is critical. Pornographic expression has limited First Amendment protection, but obscene expression has no First Amendment protection.

Obscenity laws have been in existence in the United States for most of its history. Until 1957, the First Amendment placed minimal restraints on governmental authority to regulate sexually explicit materials. *Roth v. United States* (1957) is the first modern authoritative First Amendment obscenity decision. *Roth* established a category of *un*protected speech and required the government to prove that expression fell into that category. Under *Roth*, the trier of fact had to decide "whether to the average person, applying contemporary community standards, the dominant theme of the material taken as a whole appeals to a prurient interest."[32]

Justice William Brennan identified the reason for not giving obscenity constitutional protection:

> All ideas having even the slightest redeeming social importance — unorthodox ideas, controversial ideas, even ideas hateful to the prevailing climate of opinion — have the full protection of the guaranties, unless excludable because they encroach upon the limited area of more important interests. *But implicit in the history of the First Amendment is the rejection of obscenity as utterly without redeeming social importance* [italics added].[33]

In 1973, the Supreme Court expanded the category of obscene speech by creating a new, less restrictive test in *Miller v. California*. In *Paris Adult Theater v. Slaton*, another sexual speech case decided the same day, Justice Brennan dissented. After addressing the troublesome question of defining obscenity in several cases since *Roth*, Brennan abandoned the effort to find a satisfactory legal definition for obscenity:

> The essence of our problem in the obscenity area is that we have been unable to provide "sensitive tools" to separate obscenity from other sexually oriented but constitutionally protected speech, so that efforts to suppress the former do not spill over into the suppression of the latter.[34]

Note that Brennan did not reject the category of obscenity; he merely said that the Court had not found a way to avoid vague definitions that threatened protected categories of speech. His basic premise articulated in *Roth* that some speech has no social value and therefore is outside of First Amendment protection remains unchanged.

In recent years feminist scholars, such as Cass Sunstein, Andrea Dworkin, and Catherine MacKinnon, have challenged the legal definition of obscenity and attempted to develop an alternative definition of obscenity which, if accepted by the courts, would expand the category to include pornographic speech that is now outside the legal category of obscenity.[35] The success of the feminist effort remains uncertain, but it is clear that more than 30 years after *Roth* the category of obscenity remains vague and satisfies no one.

Broadcast Doctrine

Broadcast speech is the only category of expression defined by technology. The *physical* scarcity of the broadcast spectrum is the distinguishing factor. In *National Broadcasting Co. v. FCC* (1943), the Supreme Court found that the limited physical capacity of the airwaves to carry broadcast signals required a different First Amendment standard. This "unique" aspect of broadcasting created special problems that justified government licensing and regulation of broadcasting:

> Freedom of utterance is abridged to many who wish to use the limited facilities of radio. Unlike other modes of expression, it is subject to governmental regulation.[36]

Physical scarcity remains the linchpin of First Amendment broadcast doctrine. In *Red Lion Broadcasting v. FCC* (1969), the court reaffirmed its acceptance of spectrum scarcity as a valid justification for government-mandated affirmative obligations for broadcasters to present controversial programming, and it defined the First Amendment interest in broadcasting in terms of the listeners. Justice Byron White, writing for a unanimous court, turned around the traditional view of the First Amendment as a protection for the rights of speakers:

> It is the right of the viewers and listeners, not the right of the broadcasters, which is paramount. . . . It is the right of the public to receive suitable access to social, political, esthetic, moral and other ideas and experiences which is crucial here.[37]

This focus on the right of broadcast audiences to receive a wide range of information from a diversity of sources establishes a First Amendment framework in which government content regulations such as the equal time rule and federal candidate access rules are not violations of broadcasters' right to freedom of expression. Broadcast licensees *do not* have the same First Amendment rights as speakers using other forms of mass media.

Attempts by legal scholars, such as law professor Jerome Barron and lawyer Henry Geller, to extend the logic of *Red Lion* into print, cable, and other nonbroadcast media have failed because the Supreme Court has been unwilling to ignore the physical scarcity distinction.[38] In *Miami Herald v. Tornillo* (1974), Chief Justice Warren Burger explicitly rejected the use of an *economic* scarcity justification for creating a constitutional right of access to newspapers.[39]

The use of physical scarcity as a means of distinguishing broadcasting from other media has been under increasing attack in recent years. In 1985, the FCC found as a matter of administrative law that the Fairness Doctrine no longer served the public interest because, in part, the proliferation of cable television systems and programming services and other new media eliminates scarcity as a relevant concern. The FCC repealed the Fairness Doctrine in 1987, but Congress is considering bills to reinstate it. Should that occur, the Supreme Court will have an opportunity to look once again at the question of physical scarcity and the First Amendment right of broadcasters.[40]

Commercial Speech

Under the First Amendment, commercial speech is expression proposing the buying and selling of products or services. Prior to the mid-1970s, the First Amendment placed little restriction on government regulation of commercial speech. Government could regulate offers to buy or sell products, promises concerning the performance of products, or promises of services, without raising First Amendment concerns.

In part, the lack of constitutional protection for commercial speech was the result of judges' view of the importance of commercial speech in a democracy. Judge Jerome Frank, an influential jurist on the Second Circuit Court of Appeal, wrote "Such men as Thomas Paine, John Milton and Thomas Jefferson were not fighting for the right to peddle commercial advertising." Justice Hugo Black, a strong supporter of First Amendment rights, dismissed the claim of First Amendment protection for commercial speech by saying that the First Amendment did not "apply to the merchant who goes door-to-door selling pots."[41]

However, in the mid-1970s the Supreme Court recognized limited First Amendment protection of commercial speech in cases involving state regulation of the advertising of legal abortion services, house-for-sale signs, contraceptive advertising, lawyer advertising, and advertising the availability and price of prescription drugs.[42]

As with broadcast expression, First Amendment protection of commercial speech is based on the audience's interest in receiving useful information. Therefore, government regulation of false, deceptive, or misleading commercial speech is not a violation of the First Amendment.

In a 1980 decision, *Central Hudson Gas & Electric v. Public Service Commission of New York*, the Supreme Court established a test for determining the scope of proper government regulation of truthful commercial speech about lawful products or services. While the test was initially viewed as a potentially strong protection of commercial speech, judicial use of the test and a 1986 Supreme Court decision, *Posadas de Puerto Rico Associates v. Tourism Co. of Puerto Rico*, have raised serious concerns about the protection of commercial speech under the First Amendment.[43]

FREE EXPRESSION THEORISTS

Zechariah Chafee, Jr.

Zechariah Chafee's "Freedom of Speech in Wartime," a 1919 *Harvard Law Review* article later expanded and published as *Freedom of Speech* (1920), is the first major attempt to establish a framework for thinking about freedom of the press in the 20th century. Chafee's is not the first contribution to free expression literature in the century — law professor Henry Schofield, free speech advocate Theodore Schroeder, and others had written about free expression in the pre-World War I period — but Chafee's influence on 20th-century free expression scholarship has overshadowed other early writers.

The context in which Chafee wrote is important to understanding his view. In 1919, the Supreme Court upheld convictions under the Espionage and Sedition Acts in three cases. In this climate, Chafee authored a legal brief for a more expansive interpretation of First Amendment protections and in support of Justice Holmes' clear and present danger test.

As history, Chafee's scholarship was flawed because he ignored large chunks of free expression history that did not support his thesis. However, as an articulation of a broad theory of freedom of expression in a democratic society, Chafee sounded themes that are central to liberal free expression theory:

> [The First Amendment] is a declaration of national policy in favor of the public discussion of all public questions. . . . One of the most important purposes of society and government is the discovery and spread of truth on subjects of general concern. This is possible only through absolutely unlimited discussion.[44]

Chafee did not advocate an absolute right to freedom of expression. He acknowledged the "other purposes of government" and that freedom of expression had to be balanced against other interests. But, in contrast to the dominant legal precedent and status quo political values of the time (Chafee nearly lost his Harvard Law School professorship because of his writings), he argued that free expression "ought to weigh very heavily in the scale."[45]

The importance of free expression in a democracy and the need to draw lines to reconcile free expression with other societal interests are major themes in free expression theory that are far from settled. Chafee began and framed a discourse that shows no sign of reaching closure.

Alexander Meiklejohn

In "Free Speech and Its Relation to Self-Government," the lead essay in *Political Freedom* (1948), philosopher Alexander Meiklejohn presented a theory of the First Amendment based on the concept of self-government. In a democratic society, he reasoned, the people are the governors; therefore, they must have access to all the information necessary to make informed, rational decisions concerning the governing of the society. "What is essential," Meiklejohn wrote, "is not that everyone shall speak, but that everything worth saying shall be said . . . no suggestion of policy shall be denied a hearing."[46]

The requirements of self-government provide the strongest argument for the protection of freedom of expression in Meiklejohn's view. Thus, political speech (i.e., speech concerning the political process) must have absolute protection under the First Amendment. All other speech is protected, but that protection must be balanced against other constitutional interests.

William Brennan's majority opinion in *New York Times v. Sullivan* (1964), the landmark Supreme Court decision extending First Amendment protection into libel law, relies on a Meiklejohnian view of freedom of expression. Meiklejohn's concern for protecting a broad range of discussion and debate is echoed in Brennan's often-quoted language in *Sullivan*:

> Thus we consider this case against the background of a profound national commitment to the principle that debate on public issues should be uninhibited, robust, and wide-open, and that it may well include vehement, caustic, and sometimes unpleasantly sharp attacks on government and public officials.[47]

The history of constitutional libel law since *Sullivan* demonstrates some of the problems inherent in Meiklejohnian free press theory, but, as Zechariah Chafee observed in 1948, "Meiklejohn's best contribution to the analysis of the First Amendment is his stress on the interest in self-government." [48]

Thomas I. Emerson

A comprehensive theory of freedom of expression has yet to be developed. Emerson, in "Toward a General Theory of the First Amendment" (1963), attempted to create a theory capturing all of the perspectives found in liberal free expression literature. Emerson's system is intended to accomplish four goals:

(1) a means of ensuring individual self-fulfillment;
(2) A process for discovering truth;
(3) A means of participating in decision making;
(4) A means of achieving a stable community through consensus.[49]

Emerson's work is quite valuable because he provided a comprehensive and systematic discussion of the problem of establishing a comprehensive theory of freedom of expression. He did not succeed in solving many of the conflicts inherent in the sweeping scope of his system—for example, the goals of self-fulfillment and discovering truth and *participating* in decision making are not always compatible—but he does provide a means for sorting out the conflicts.

Harry Kalven, Jr.

Where the goal of most legal theorists is to find unifying principles and theories with broad application, Harry Kalven cautioned against the fashioning of a general theory of freedom of expression while at the same time recognizing the importance of free expression in a democracy.[50]

Kalven looked for the meaning of freedom of expression in the particular kinds of issues litigated under the First Amendment and only then attempted to draw general principles about freedom of expression. Kalven's report that Alexander Meiklejohn said *New York Times v. Sullivan* was "an occasion for dancing in the streets," and his discussion of the "central meaning of the First Amendment" in the 1964 *Supreme Court Review* made explicit the link between Justice Brennan's landmark opinion in *Sullivan* and the free expression philosophy of Meiklejohn.[51]

Kalven viewed the question of freedom of expression as more than a question of legal theory or philosophical principle. It was a question of sociology as well as of law. As a common law scholar, Kalven was accustomed to watching the evolution of law as courts confronted similar but different legal questions shaped by different fact situations and attempted to apply legal principles. The principles changed as a result of the process. Kalven recognized the importance of this process to the law of freedom of expression. In *A Worthy Tradition* (1988), published after his death, Kalven traces the "tradition" of freedom of expression in 20th-century law and in doing so, crafts an intricate web of free expression theories.

The Current Ferment

While freedom of the press issues have been litigated throughout the history of the United States, and the First Amendment litigation has been an important issue since 1919, most of the theoretical writing about freedom of the press has been done in the past 15 to 20 years. The writings of Chafee, Meiklejohn, Emerson, and Kalven set the stage for current thinking about freedom of the press, but it is fair to say that they provide only a point of departure and important counterpoints for efforts to fashion workable theories of freedom of expression. The authors discussed are merely the tip of a large body of important contemporary writing.

In reading the brief summaries below, note that the authors are not concerned primarily with original intent. They all agree that the task is to develop a theoretical framework for understanding freedom of expression that respects and is in agreement with the intent and text of the First

Amendment, but they recognize that interpretation of broadly worded constitutional texts is a process of making choices. These theorists are concerned with finding a way to make the best choice.

Ronald Dworkin

In *Taking Rights Seriously* (1978) and several other important books, Ronald Dworkin has fashioned a rights-based philosophy of law in which he defines and defends a liberal theory of law. Central to his theory is the principle that individual rights are fundamental and should in all but extreme circumstances be protected, even when allowing that the individual freedom may harm the public good. Individual rights, in Dworkin's theory, "trump" over perceived public interests because the fundamental goal of a liberal society is to protect and enhance individual freedoms.[52]

In a series of essays collected in *A Matter of Principle* (1985), he addresses several free expression questions. He cautions against overreaching theories of freedom of expression and argues for a "principle of free speech" that would protect the core values of free expression. A principle of free expression argues that "a particular rule is necessary in order to protect an individual right that some person (or group) has against other people, or against the society or government as a whole."[53]

If free expression is viewed as a matter of principle, then arguments for special protections for the press because of the public good served by the press will fail. But as Dworkin and others such as William Van Alstyne have shown, the claim of special privilege carries with it the obligation of special responsibility. Dworkin's rights-based theory of freedom of expression limits the scope of the right, but provides a stronger base for free expression arguments.[54]

Lee C. Bollinger

Speech is a form of behavior. In *The Tolerant Society*, law professor Lee Bollinger begins by rejecting the speech/action distinction in free expression theory and law. Speech is a form of social behavior which is open to regulation. The task, he argues, is to develop a "social principle of free speech."[55] In attempting to develop a free expression theory, Bollinger addresses three questions:

(1) Why should we exercise such extraordinary self-restraint in the regulation of speech, when we do not with respect to nonspeech behavior?
(2) Why . . . should we tolerate extremist speech?

(3) Why should we vest the interpretative and enforcement functions of the principle in the judicial branch?[56]

A "general tolerance theory" is the result of Bollinger's efforts. He attempts to develop a theory that captures not only the classical ideas of speech as a means of preserving democratic government and as an exercise of individual freedom, but also the value of expression in understanding self and developing intellectual capacity.

This theory, as Bollinger notes, is not an end point in the search for free expression theory, but as is the case with an earlier Bollinger article, "Freedom of the Press and Public Access: Toward a Theory of Partial Regulation," it challenges long-held assumptions about freedom of expression and asks us to think about old problems in new ways.[57]

Martin Redish

Free expression theorists, Martin Redish wrote in *Freedom of Expression: A Critical Analysis* (1984), "must seek general guidelines of interpretation that simultaneously provide the strong deference to free speech interests that the language and the policies of the First Amendment command while allowing the judiciary the case-by-case flexibility necessary to reconcile those interests with truly compelling and conflicting societal concerns."[58]

The goal is to ensure that "the interchange of ideas, information and suggestions is . . . kept free and open, at least if the interchange presents no real threat of harm to society." The task is to develop an overarching principle that will provide maximum protection for expression.[59]

Redish labels his first principle "individual self-realization." He chose this vague term because it allows him to capture both the personal value of a right to freedom of expression and the broader social values achieved when an individual is free to play an active role in shaping the social and political world.

This broad normative value (individuals should have the right to self-realization) allows the theorist to capture a wide range of more narrowly defined values.

Cass R. Sunstein

In a 1986 *Duke Law Journal* article, Sunstein crafted a feminist argument for broader government power to regulate pornographic expression. Building on the work of other feminist legal scholars such as Catherine

MacKinnon, she attacked the most difficult hurdle confronting regulation of pornography — it is regulation based on the *viewpoint* of the speaker — and concluded that pornography can be regulated without violating First Amendment principles if it is agreed that "pornography produces significant harms and that these harms cannot be alleviated through public debate alone."[60]

Sunstein's work is representative of the influence of critical scholarship on First Amendment theory. Courts have yet to accept the feminist critique of pornography, but the critique has changed significantly the debate over regulation of sexually explicit expression.

Summary

Giving meaning to "congress shall make no law . . . abridging freedom of speech, or of the press" has never been a simple task. This chapter presents an overview of the theoretical approaches used by free expression theorists and the judiciary in attempting to create principled, consistent definitions of freedom of expression.

The researcher interested in communication and law requires a basic map of free expression theory. The map just viewed provides a few landmarks but leaves discovery of much of the detail to the reader.

NOTES

1. Harry Kalven, Jr., *The Negro and the First Amendment* (Columbus, 1965): 5.

2. For accounts of the Rushdie affair see "A 'Satanic' Fury," *Newsweek* (27 February 1989): 34; "Differing Voices on 'Verses,' " *The San Francisco Chronicle* (24 February 1989): B1, 5.

3. For discussion of state constitution free press clauses, "Symposium: The Emergence of State Constitutional Law," *Texas Law Review* 63 (1985): 959; Ronald K.L. Collins, "Foreword: Reliance on State Constitutions," *University of Puget Sound Law Review* 8 (1984): vi; Kenneth Alan Schiffler, "Fifty-One First Amendments," M.A. thesis (University of Washington, 1986); Emile Netzhammer, "State Constitutions as Sources of Expanded Protection of Freedom of Expression," doctoral dissertation (University of Utah, 1987).

4. Miller v. California, 413 U.S. 15, 24 (1973); in Pope v. Illinois, 481 U.S. 497 (1987), the Court modified the third part of the Miller test by adding a reasonable person standard.

5. 413 U.S. 15, 34–36 (1973).

6. State v. Henry, 732 P.2d 9, 17 (Or. 1987).

7. Lee C. Bollinger, *The Tolerant Society* (New York, 1986): 6; Martin H. Redish, *Freedom of Expression* (Charlottesville, Va., 1984): 2.

8. Bollinger, *Tolerant Society*, 128.

9. Hustler Magazine v. Falwell, 108 S.Ct. 876 (1988).

10. Abrams v. United States, 250 U.S. 616, 630 (1919).

11. See, for example, Irving Brant, *The Bill of Rights* (Indianapolis, 1965); Vincent Blasi, "The Checking Value in First Amendment Theory," *American Bar Foundation Research Journal* (1977): 521.

12. Leonard W. Levy, *Emergence of a Free Press* (New York, 1985): xi; an enlarged and revised edition of *Legacy of Suppression* (New York, 1960).

13. Jeffery A. Smith, *Printers and Press Freedom* (New York, 1988); David A. Anderson, "The Origins of the Press Clause," *UCLA Law Review* 30 (1983): 455.

14. Wm. David Sloan and Thomas Schwartz, "Freedom of the Press, 1690–1801," *American Journalism* 5 (1988): 176.

15. Schenck v. United States, 249 U.S. 47, 52 (1919). Jeremy Cohen suggests, however, the jurisprudence of the time and deference to legislative intent prevented Holmes from any serious consideration of the First Amendment in Schenck; see Cohen, *Congress Shall Make No Law* (Ames, Iowa, 1989).

16. Zechariah Chafee, Jr., *Freedom of Speech* (New York, 1920); *Freedom of Speech in the United States* (Cambridge, Mass., 1941): 81, 82.

17. For example, see Redish, *Freedom of Expression*, 173; Frank R. Strong, "Fifty Years of 'Clear and Present Danger,' " *The Supreme Court Review* (1969): 41; Hans A. Linde, " 'Clear and Present Danger' Reexamined," *Stanford Law Review* 22 (1970): 1163.

18. Everette E. Dennis, Donald M. Gillmor, and David L. Gray, *Justice Hugo Black and the First Amendment* (Ames, Iowa, 1978); Haig Bosmajian, *Justice Douglas and Freedom of Speech* (Metuchen, N.J., 1980).

19. Dennis v. United States, 341 U.S. 494, 585 (1951).

20. Terminiello v. Chicago, 337 U.S. 1, 4 (1949).

21. Hugo L. Black, "The Bill of Rights," *New York University Law Review* 35 (1960): 865.

22. Cohen v. California, 403 U.S. 15, 16–26 (1970).

23. Ibid., 27.

24. Franklyn S. Haiman, *Speech and Law in a Free Society* (Chicago, 1981): 38.

25. See Pruneyard Shopping Center v. Robins, 447 U.S. 74 (1980) and Hudgens v. NLRB, 424 U.S. 507 (1976) for U.S. Supreme Court decisions on this question. For state decisions, see, for example, Alderwood Associates v. Washington Environmental Council, 635 P. 2d 108 (Wa. 1981); Shad Alliance v. Smith Haven Mall, 488 N.E. 2d 1211 (N.Y. 1985).

26. United States v. Carolene Products, 304 U.S. 144, 152, ftn. 4 (1938).

27. New York Times Co. v. United States; United States v. Washington Post, 713 U.S. 403 (1971).

28. New York Times v. Sullivan, 376 U.S. 254 (1964).

29. For histories of privacy law see Don R. Pember, *Privacy and the Press* (Seattle, 1972); Richard F. Hixon, *Privacy in a Public Society* (New York, 1987).

30. Time, Inc. v. Hill, 385 U.S. 374 (1967).

31. Jacobellis v. Ohio, 378 U.S. 184, 197 (1964).

32. Roth v. United States, 354 U.S. 476, 488–89 (1957).

33. Ibid., 484.

34. Paris Adult Theater v. Slaton, 413 U.S. 49, 79–80 (1973).

35. Cass R. Sunstein, "Pornography and the First Amendment," *Duke Law Journal* (1986): 589; Catherine MacKinnon, *Feminism Unmodified* (Cambridge, Mass., 1987); Andrea Dworkin, *Pornography* (New York, 1981).

36. National Broadcasting Co. v. FCC, 319 U.S. 190, 226 (1943).

37. Red Lion Broadcasting v. FCC, 395 U.S. 367, 290 (1969).

38. Jerome Barron, "Access to the Press—A New First Amendment Right," *Harvard Law Review* 80 (1967): 1641; Henry Geller, "Communication Law—A Half Century Later," *Federal Communication Law Journal* 37 (1985): 73.

39. Miami Herald v. Tornillo, 418 U.S. 241 (1974).

40. Fairness Report, 102 FCC 2d 143 (1985); "The Decline and Fall of the Fairness Doctrine," *Broadcasting* (10 August 1987): 1.

41. Chrestensen v. Valentine, 122 F. 2d 511, 524 (2nd Cir. 1941); Breard v. City of Alexandria, 341 U.S. 622, 650 (1951).

42. Bigelow v. Virginia, 421 U.S. 809 (1975); Virginia State Board of Pharmacy v. Virginia Consumer Council, 425 U.S. 748 (1976); Linmark Association v. City of Willingboro, 431 U.S. 85 (1977); Carey v. Population Services International, 431 U.S. 678 (1977); Bates v. State Bar of Arizona, 433 U.S. 350 (1977).

43. Central Hudson Gas & Electric v. Public Service Commission of New York, 447 U.S. 557 (1980); Posadas de Puerto Rico Associates v. Tourism Co. of Puerto Rico, 478 U.S. 328 (1986).

44. Zechariah Chafee, Jr., "Freedom of Speech in Wartime," *Harvard Law Review* 32 (1919): 934, 956.

45. Ibid., 957.

46. Alexander Meiklejohn, *Political Freedom* (New York, 1948): 26–27.

47. 376 U.S. 254, 270 (1964).

48. Zechariah Chafee, "Book Review: Alexander Meiklejohn's Free Speech and Its Relation to Self Government," *Harvard Law Review* 62 (1949): 96.

49. Thomas I. Emerson, *The System of Freedom of Expression* (New York, 1970): 6–7; "Toward a General Theory of the First Amendment," *Yale Law Journal* (1963): 877.

50. Harry Kalven, Jr., *A Worthy Tradition* (New York, 1988): 3; *The Negro and the First Amendment* (Columbus, 1965): 6.

51. Harry Kalven, Jr., "The New York Times Case: A Note on 'The Central Meaning of the First Amendment,' " *The Supreme Court Review* (1964): 125, 191.

52. Ronald Dworkin, *Taking Rights Seriously* (Cambridge, Mass., 1978).

53. Ronald Dworkin, *A Matter of Principle* (Cambridge, Mass., 1985): 375.

54. William Van Alstyne, *Interpretations of the First Amendment* (Durham, N.C. 1984).

55. Bollinger, *The Tolerant Society*, 107.

56. Ibid., 39–40.

57. Lee C. Bollinger, "Freedom of the Press and Public Access: Toward a Theory of Partial Regulation," *Michigan Law Review* (1976): 1.

58. Redish, *Freedom of Expression*, 3.

59. Ibid., 85.

60. Sunstein, "Pornography," 589.

4

A SOCIAL RESEARCH APPROACH
TO LIBEL

A communication and law approach to libel involves First Amendment theory, torts, the sociology of libel litigation, the sociology of libel law, and communication theory. Together they allow for theory generation in law, in freedom of expression, and in communication that provides insight unavailable from any single perspective.

Libel litigation has provided the backdrop for a wide range of social, political, and even Hollywood drama. The landmark *New York Times v. Sullivan* spawned the constitutionalization of libel law in a Supreme Court decision delivered over the death wail of southern school segregation.[1] *Westmoreland v. CBS* matched the retired commander of United States troops in Vietnam against the broadcast news group that publicly judged the war a stalemate.[2] Ironically, *Westmoreland*, too, was mired in a stalemate both in the courtroom and out: one more confrontation, one more surrogate political contest between hawks and doves, policy makers and citizen critics. And for the public there was Paul Newman and Sally Field in Hollywood's version of libel, love, and litigation — *Absence of Malice* — and Carol Burnett in a real life suit against the *National Enquirer* after the tabloid claimed the actress poured wine over the head of Secretary of State Henry Kissinger.[3]

At first blush the bulk of the analyses of these cases and others fits the traditional case law research approach and focuses attention on litigation strategies. Other research about libel, however, is also available. A review of some of these approaches to libel, what we come to know from them and how we come to know — outside of litigation strategy analysis — provides examples of social research in communication and law. And it makes possible a consideration of the relations among libel law, freedom of expression, and communication for the communication scholar interested in communication and law.

For purposes of discussion, we begin our case study of libel as a substantive area of communication and law by subdividing libel itself into five conceptual types. Within each quintile we can examine representative research. Finally, we can look for ways to integrate the five areas with the goal of theory construction.

FIRST AMENDMENT THEORY

The civil rights movements spilled over throughout the 1950s and 1960s from college campuses and southern churches onto the pages and television screens of the national media. The landmark *New York Times v. Sullivan* (1964) began with a paid advertisement supporting Martin Luther King, Jr. and the civil rights movement. In essence, the ad implied King was harassed by local government officials. Was Montgomery, Alabama Commissioner L.B. Sullivan libeled by the *Times*?

Libel law was based at the time on common law rather than on a uniform federal rule, and the general rule was strict liability.[4] A defendant who published false, defamatory facts was liable — regardless of extenuating circumstances or intent. The Supreme Court plucked from this environment a defamation suit and as Harry Kalven, Jr., a law professor and First Amendment theorist, points out, identified and developed "a new genre of First Amendment problem."[5]

Kalven found in *Times v. Sullivan* an attempt to develop a theory of the First Amendment cognizant of the framers' intended meaning. The case *was* a libel case. Yet the Court's unanimous opinion was built upon a foundation of First Amendment theory developed well outside the realm of libel law — and not by an attorney but by a philosopher, Alexander Meiklejohn.[6] *New York Times v. Sullivan* developed First Amendment theory from a *philosophic theory*, that is, a theory of freedom of expression rather than a theory of law, per se. The Court considered democratic theory and constitutional theory viewed within the historical context of the 1798 Sedition Act. The sedition law failed the test of public support, but until 1964 its ghost flourished — never directly challenged in the Supreme Court and tacitly ignored in the World War I sedition cases such as *Schenck* and *Debs* and *Abrams*.[7] For Kalven, the central meaning of the First Amendment located the *right* to discuss public issues as the core of the First Amendment — a tenet abused in the past by judicial tests and doctrines such as clear and present danger and ad hoc balancing that were developed in the World War I sedition cases. Examining constitutional history *and* law *and* freedom of expression Kalven concluded,

We get a sense of difference between a legal theory of freedom of speech and a philosophic theory as we trace the career of seditious libel from seventeenth-century England through Fox's Libel Act through the Sedition Act to the *Times* case. . . . We are reminded not only of how much more complex the legal debate over freedom of speech or over seditious libel can be, but again of the arresting problem how much freedom of speech in a legal system must depend on law's conscious distrust of its own process to make needed discriminations.

The closing question, of course, is whether the treatment of seditious libel as the key concept for development of appropriate constitutional doctrine will prove germinal. . . . The invitation to follow a dialectic progression from public official to government policy to public policy to matters of public domain, like art, seems to me overwhelming. If the Court accepts the invitation it will slowly work out for itself the theory of free speech Alexander Meiklejohn has been offering us for some fifteen years now.[8]

Kalven's theoretical approach does not ignore courtroom strategy. Nor does it end there. He employs case analysis, historiography, and an integration of philosopher Meiklejohn's theorizing on the Constitution and democracy. The mix produces a developing theory of the First Amendment that may be arrived at only with an approach that does not consign the Constitution to the exclusive proprietary arena of the attorney.

Kalven's work is presented not because his approach is unique. Law, and especially constitutional law, often melds history, case law, and democratic theory. Rather, Kalven is an exemplar of the research and theory construction in one area of our conceptual map of the *communication and law* approach to libel. Research and theory construction in this landscape recognize multiple methodological and conceptual approaches. First Amendment theory here is based on a philosophic understanding of freedom of expression and on history, as much as on traditional jurisprudence.

It is no secret that what has come to be known — derogatorily — as *law office* or *courtroom history* is often one-sided history.[9] Constitutional historian Leonard Levy gives the Court failing marks and finds that over its own 200-year history the historical abilities of the justices "might charitably be described as historical incompetence."[10] Nonetheless, the integration of history and law can and does provide new perspective and new theory — for those who will begin with an a priori assumption that the researcher must be properly aware of the mores and operating codes of each of the disciplines he borrows from. Kalven recognized, for example, the line between tort and constitutional law. "For the torts teacher," he wrote, the *Times* case "has the dizzying consequence of transmuting a part of his domain — one that he traditionally does not reach until the last day of the semester—into constitutional law, the Valhalla of the law school curriculum."[11] With similar care we must distinguish between constitutional law and history and philosophy, even as we work to pour a mortar mixed from all three.

New York Times v. Sullivan provided the Court, and Kalven, an exemplar of seditious libel with its clear implications for freedom of expression. Inextricably interwoven with the tort-based defamation of an individual public official was a constitutional question of seditious libel. Criticism of the man and of the government policy were inseparable. Together they comprised Kalven's new genre of First Amendment question. The occasion presented the Court with an opportunity for theory construction which recognized the need to operationalize theory to meet fact. It also presented the need to cross disciplinary boundaries. The result was the creation of the federal actual malice rule.

It is possible for the attorney to conduct First Amendment research strictly from the confines of case law. Yet as Kalven knew, the researcher interested in theory needs to go beyond precedent and black letter law. And, as Kalven recognized in *New York Times v. Sullivan*, the courtroom is not always limited to black letter law with its string citations and narrow lines of legal reasoning. *Times v. Sullivan* spawned scores of legal journal articles focusing on jurisprudence. It also spawned consideration of history and the social and constitutional roles of communication—considerations well-suited to the communication researcher.

TORTS

A tort, defined in *Black's Law Dictionary*, is a "private or civil wrong or injury, other than a breach of contract, for which the court will provide a remedy in the form of an action for damages."[12] For the communication or journalism researcher the area usually begins and ends with libel and privacy and focuses on the legal claims of individuals who allege injury by the press. Of the 15 articles appearing in *Journalism Quarterly* from 1984 through 1988 that focused on libel, 13 were based on a case law analysis of the libel tort. Three issues underlie much of the research: What are the origins of its elements; how is libel litigated; and how is libel likely to be litigated in the future?

The intense interest in the application of libel law to reporters, publishers, and fiction writers is natural for journalism and communication researchers. Yet the question lingers—what distinguishes this line of research from legal research conducted by attorneys less interested in communication and journalism, per se, and more interested in the law? The answer for the most part is, very little. In fact, there is a paucity of tort-related research that goes beyond the litigation strategy and guideline-for-the-journalist approach. Communication researchers, with few exceptions, have done little to carve out a distinct research agenda identifiable as their own discipline.

There are some exceptions. Ronald Farrar's very useful examination of the libel tort, "News Councils and Libel Actions,"[13] is addressed below in the section titled "The Sociology of Libel." Other works such as the survey research offered by James Bow and Ben Silver, attempt to document a chilling effect brought on by libel.[14]

Also notable is David Anderson's 1985 examination of the libel tort after *Times v. Sullivan*. Although "Presumed Harm: An Item for the Unfinished Agenda of *Times v. Sullivan*" was a traditional and very well-crafted analysis of the libel tort by the University of Texas law professor, Anderson's research raised issues that appear tailor-made for the communication scholar.[15] Anderson attacked the ability of the *Times* rule to protect open expression sufficiently. "The experience of the last twenty years has shown that as long as there is a potential windfall at the end of the tunnel, plaintiffs will continue to litigate despite whatever doctrinal obstacles may be placed in their way,"[16] Anderson concluded. If constitutional obstacles could be hurdled, then Anderson suggested a barrier more formidable: "The only way to stop the escalation is limit the stakes, and the place to start is by insisting on some proof of injury."[17] As we'll see below in our discussion of communication effects, Anderson's call for proof of injury raises questions well within a communication research agenda.

Robert Drechsel, a professor of mass communication and journalism at the University of Wisconsin, Madison, has been especially active as a communication researcher interested in torts. Drechsel has identified at least two troublesome torts involving the media—a close cousin of the libel and privacy torts known as emotional distress, and suits against the media for publication of information allegedly causing physical damage.[18]

Drechsel points out that "Without recognition of a legal duty owed by defendant to a plaintiff, and without evidence that breach of that duty caused the plaintiff's harm, there can be no negligence liability. Consequently, for the boundaries of such tort liability to expand, courts must be persuaded to recognize new legal duties."[19] Recognition, Drechsel warns, may find support in two forms: media ethics codes and mass communication research. Bench-bar-press guidelines or professional organization codes of conduct might make it possible to claim an identifiable duty to sources or readers. Communication research may make possible the claim that a publisher should have expected a particular damaging effect from his printed or broadcast message. Drechsel concludes,

> In writing and talking ethics, the media would be wise consistently to empha-size what may not be sufficiently obvious — that espousal of ethical standards is not forfeiture of legal rights, that moral ideals are not inherently legal impera-tives. And as the question of factual causation becomes less problematic, ques-tions of public policy — most particularly the question of the social utility of certain types of expression — will be of paramount importance.[20]

Drechsel's research raises, within the realm of tort theory and practice, questions of interest beyond litigation strategy. These are issues of com-munication effects and media sociology well within the main currents of communication — rather than only legal — research.

Another area of torts receiving increased attention is the privacy claim of false light. States such as Ohio and North Carolina have refused to recognize the tort. For those in communication studies the first step re-quires traditional legal analysis of the type undertaken by journalism pro-fessors Ruth Walden and Emile Netzhammer.[21] What are the courts doing with regard to the four privacy torts and how does this affect mass media practitioners?

The next step will require a theoretical approach beyond the identifica-tion of legal norms. True, we need to understand torts — their application, their construction, their place in the law. But we also need to keep in mind that in and of itself we could never claim that torts are a distinct area of communication research. They are an area of law. They are taught and studied in law schools, not in communication schools. Because they im-pact on communication we must study torts as lawyers study torts. We should, however, limit our time as communication researchers in an area clearly within the domain of law. Our interest is communication and jour-nalism. Our task is to develop a clear research agenda within the disci-pline of *communication and law*.

SOCIOLOGY OF LITIGATION

Closely related to tort and constitutional research is an area we will distinguish as the *sociology of litigation*. Here we are interested in a macro approach to libel. Constitutional and tort research by and large take a micro approach, focusing on the substance of individual cases and depending for their methodology on case analysis. Our focus now is on such broad questions as: What kinds of cases go to trial? How often do plaintiffs win? Can we identify patterns in the legal or judicial institutions bearing on our understanding of libel?

Law professor Marc Franklin analyzed 534 libel cases decided between 1976 and mid-1979 and then conducted a follow-up study of 291 additional cases.[22] His findings tell us something about policy as well as law in their panoramic portrait of libel.

We learn, for example, that despite the *Times* and *Gertz* rules, state defenses continue to play a major role in the settlement of libel cases. We learn that while plaintiffs fare well with juries, they are repeatedly defeated at the appeals level. We learn also that media defendants seldom lose appeals filed by plaintiffs, a fact suggesting a possible problem at the trial level. Franklin also identifies the importance of federalized libel rules, especially at the summary judgment stage.

What distinguishes Franklin's empirical approach from tort and constitutional studies of case law? Franklin in fact uses individual cases as his unit of analysis, which in turn allows him to examine specific litigation strategies and legal rules. His systematic examination of libel litigation as a whole, however, allows him to make conclusions that go beyond individual fact situations. Franklin asks: "Is there another area of law in which so few cases settle and in which plaintiffs who do litigate win such a small percentage of their cases?"[23] He answers with a question of policy: "In the face of determined and successful legal resistance from defendants, might a state conclude that the efforts expanded in this area were nonproductive — and abolish or stringently restrict the [libel] action?"[24]

F. Dennis Hale, a professor of journalism, took a different tack in his study of the sociology of libel litigation. Hale analyzed each of the libel decisions of the Warren and Burger Courts. Presenting his findings at the 1988 meeting of AEJMC, Hale found that "libel defendants won 87 percent of the time under Warren, compared to 45 percent under Burger"[25] Did Hale find proof that the Burger Court in fact held an antipress bias? "It was not that simple," Hale said, "this disparity in libel resulted in part from differences in the composition of the cases. The Burger Court considered more cases from the outer limits of protected speech."[26] In fact, Hale found, more than three quarters of the Warren Court cases involved criticism of elected or important government officials, while only about one third of the cases before the Burger Court fell into this constitutionally protected category.

Hale's empirical analysis carefully points out the danger of box score approaches to tabulations of judicial decision making, and it adds to our understanding of the development of libel law.

Anderson's empirical study of High Court decisions, conducted while he was a Fellow at the Gannett Center for Media Studies, went far beyond libel in its analysis of all media cases to go before the Justices over a 195-year period dating from 1791–1986.[27] Nonetheless, Anderson found that libel is second only to prior restraint in terms of decisions for the press. Again, however, the empirical finding requires context that Anderson supplies. He counsels against relying on the High Court for media protection.

"An assumption that the Supreme Court generally or historically is solicitous of media interests would be misguided; nor can one assume that an unsolicitous court must be an aberration that will right itself when some new justices are appointed," Anderson says. Overall, Anderson found the Court "less favorable to media than to the general run of litigants."[28]

Finally, Anderson's survey of media decisions allows him to question some widely held beliefs about the role the courts take in defending freedom of expression. He equates reliance on the judiciary by the media with media skepticism about legislative relief and media belief in the judicial First Amendment shield. But, warns Anderson, the overall record of the courts may not support such a stance. It may be that the media in fact need palliatives in addition to the First Amendment to ensure the functioning of a philosophic theory of freedom of expression.

A short synthesis paper by Indiana telecommunications professor Linda Lawson also deserves mention for the important approach it suggests. The articles discussed so far focus on the arguments and results used in libel litigation. Lawson turns our attention to another aspect of libel litigation — jury instructions.[29]

Descriptive studies such as Franklin's, Lawson points out, tell us that as much as 80% of the time juries rule in favor of plaintiffs. Yet the majority of such decisions are overturned on appellate review. Why? Lawson hypothesizes that the folk wisdom is inaccurate — it is not a simple question of public anger toward the media finding vent among the venire. She searches important cases and finds a repeated phenomenon: judges questioning the ability of the jury to cope with jury instructions.

Lawson does not take her notion through empirical testing, but she does identify a problem and sets the stage for useful research based on her literature review. And her essay suggests an area especially appropriate for communication-oriented study.

THE SOCIOLOGY OF LIBEL

Social research about libel extends well beyond the processes of litigation strategy and appellate jurisprudence. Researchers are now examining the *functions* of libel law with an eye toward the threshold question: Do libel law and the legal institution from which it springs accomplish what they are supposed to accomplish? What do plaintiffs expect from libel law and what do they actually receive, given the long understood fact that libel plaintiffs rarely succeed?

"Defamation," declares law professor Jerome Skolnick in the foreword to a recent symposium on libel, "is a distinctively sociological tort."[30] Skolnick points out the tort's focus on "the individual's projection of self in a society," a phenomenon complicated because individuals "constitute themselves in various milieus — business associations, communities, families — and in differing ways."[31] He identifies four areas needing comprehensive analysis under his scheme: the social history of defamation; conceptions of what law is supposed to accomplish; media practices and policies developed in reaction to law; and the impact of defamation law on litigation and the trial courts.

Taking part in the same symposium, law professor Robert Post suggests still another conceptualization of defamation — one that considers reputation not as a single concept, but as three distinct notions: honor, dignity, and property. Post calls for the reassessment of "the relationship between the protection of reputation as property and the tort of injurious falsehood."[32] Post's concern is with the function of libel law. Given the haphazard conceptualizations of defamation as law, is the defamation tort in fact dysfunctional? "The role of damages in protecting reputation as dignity requires reappraisal," Post says, "as do the limitations and desirability of using courts to maintain community identity and cohesion through the enforcement of rules of civility."[33]

Sociologist Robert Bellah brings still another perspective — one that views the reputation of public officials as more than a personal possession. Bellah conceptualizes the reputation of public officials as a *public* good that serves as a cohesive fabric within society. Reputation, Bellah says, "is not a property or possession of individuals — it is a relation between persons."[34]

In effect, Post, Skolnick, and Bellah examine the basic building block of defamation—the concept of reputation. Focusing on defamation law outside of the rules of courtroom advocacy, their research suggests that the purely legal view of defamation is too restricted. They are not alone. A seminal study at the University of Iowa which analyzed 10 years of libel cases, surveyed plaintiffs and defendants, and examined media organizations raises very basic issues.[35]

The Iowa Study, as it has come to be known, raises the specter—this time from empirical investigation—that libel law does not meet many of the needs we assume it should meet. The study's findings, says law professor Randall Bezanson, "paint a picture of legal doctrine and constitutional theory that bears only the most tenuous relationship to the actual conduct and motives of the parties to the suit."[36]

Courts do not and cannot consider the relationship of the laws they uphold to the social results enforcement of those laws are intended to bring about. A judge who believes at the personal level that the death penalty is not a deterrent to murder nonetheless must still enforce the law as it *is* rather than as he conceives it *should* be.

What *should* libel law be? The Iowa Study began with the recognition of four assumptions embedded in law: (1) Reputations are harmed by words and protected by libel law; (2) much of the harm results in monetary damages, and plaintiffs generally are most interested in recovering those financial losses; (3) the final decision in libel adjudication reflects the plaintiff's claim of harm to reputation from the publication of false statements; and (4) constitutional protections such as the actual malice rule protect the press and discourage some kinds of suits. The Iowa group, however, found just the opposite. None of their starting point assumptions about the functioning of libel law "adequately reflect the real world of libel litigation."[37]

The advantage of social research such as the Iowa Study is obvious. Released from the needs of litigation strategy, Bezanson, journalism professor Gilbert Cranberg, and mass communication professor John Soloski are able to focus on basic questions of the relations among law, communication, and behavior. Their findings suggest that people sue the media not because of fiscal harm or the potential for a financial windfall, but because of emotional suffering resulting from stories plaintiffs perceive as false. The study found that 90% of plaintiffs eventually lose. Yet plaintiffs continue to sue. Why? The answer probably lies in the emotional basis of the harm suffered and the emotional reward available in a court of law. "Plaintiffs do not have to sue to win; they can win by suing,"[38] says

Bezanson. In essence, the process of litigation provides a catharsis of sorts for the plaintiff who suffered some form of emotional trauma caused by the defamatory media coverage. For the plaintiff, it is irrelevant whether the factual situation of the immediate case provides the basis for an ultimately successful libel suit. The process of the suit provides for vindication.

For the Iowa group, the social cost of libel litigation and its inefficiency suggest new alternatives. The bottom line is the Iowa conclusion that the law doesn't get at the real motive people have for suing — and that is, clearing their names. In the end, the Iowa group suggests policy reform based on arbitration to "name clearing" as a primary function, rather than on civil litigation with its emphasis on fault.

A thoughtful essay by Indiana University journalism professor David Pritchard lends support.[39] Pritchard begins with the question: Why do people sue for libel? Many people are unhappy with media stories, yet only some initiate legal action.

Pritchard looks for his answer in a communication notion known as "disputing behavior." Based on a small, exploratory study, he found people acting on their unhappiness with stories about themselves in a variety of ways ranging from calls for clarification and retraction to libel suit threats.

Pritchard's subjects were not libel plaintiffs. Nonetheless, his interviews generate support for the theory that potential libel plaintiffs do not reach a critical threshold at which only a lawsuit will provide satisfaction unless the offending story damaged relations with "meaningful others." The study relies on subjects who are dissatisfied with errors in stories rather than with defamation — but it continues the pursuit of the question raised by others: What functions do libel suits play for plaintiffs?

A 1986 conference at the Gannett Center for Media Studies took still another view of the sociology of libel, this time focusing on its *economic cost*.[40] The sessions were meant to raise questions rather than to provide a definitive analysis of costs. The questions ranged over a broad landscape of issues involving the cost of libel insurance, the potential for editorial chilling effects, the inefficiency of litigation, and the need for increased attention to press ethics. Again, the important factor for those interested in *communication and law* is the attention given to libel concerns arising outside of the courtroom arena. Clearly, the libel debate is of concern beyond law journal litigation pursuits.

Journalism professor Ronald Farrar added still another perspective to the debate in 1986 with an essay in *Journalism Quarterly* focusing on the potential of news councils as a nonlitigation means of meeting the needs of both plaintiffs and defendants.[41]

Studies of the sociology of libel are increasing, yet at best it can be said that this approach is in its infancy. Even so, research such as the Iowa effort is cited with increasing frequency by those convinced that the overall approach to libel in the United States is in need of reform.

A major reform proposal was unveiled in 1988 by the Libel Reform Project, a group brought together by the Annenberg Washington Program.[42] It is ironic that the project's core staff consisted entirely of attorneys. It is understandable that attorneys are interested in the drafting of proposed statutes. The staff makeup also points out, however, the urgency for interdisciplinary approaches if future policy decisions involving communication are to consider adequately the wide spectrum of information that can be made available and that is relevant to the libel debate.

COMMUNICATION

Few courtroom jousts have seen volleys of communication research hurled as irrefutable evidence. Social science in the courtroom in general traces its origins to the 1908 development of the Brandeis brief in *Muller v. Oregon*. Scientific disciplines, such as psychology, that are far "older" than communication were instrumental in such landmark decisions as *Brown v. Board of Education* (1954) more than three decades ago. Nonetheless, communication research is not unknown in the legal community.

Courts in Georgia and Texas have been asked to accept public opinion surveys as evidence of community standards in obscenity prosecutions.[43] A 1983 law review comment by Suzanne Bonamici argued persuasively for the use of survey evidence in deceptive advertising cases.[44] Public opinion survey evidence has become a popular tool in trademark infringement cases.[45] And although there is little evidence of incorporation by the courts, there is a seemingly insatiable appetite among communication researchers to experiment with mock juries and otherwise empirically investigate the relationship of jury integrity to freewheeling press coverage. As Chapter 5 discusses in some detail, communication research has played an important evidential role in judicial policy decisions to open courtrooms to electronic news gathering.

The libel arena has only recently garnered the attention of communication researchers interested in communication theory and an empirical approach that extends beyond the systematic charting of judicial trends used in studies of the sociology of litigation and the sociology of libel. In part the lack of attention may be accounted for by the makeup of the libel tort itself. Libel consists of four elements: identification, publication, defamation, and fault.[46] The first three elements relate directly to the question of whether a reputation has been damaged, thereby raising an issue of tort law. Here, the interest is in the individual's legal interest in reputation. The fault element has nothing to do with reputation. The constitutionally-mandated end of strict liability in libel is simply a recognition of the societal interest in a robust and uninhibited marketplace of ideas. Yet as Anderson and others point out, 90% of a libel trial involves not questions of damage to reputation, but the determination of fault. The research has followed this trend.

Newtonian Communication

Entertainer Wayne Newton's libel action against NBC included a good deal of novel attention to the reputational side of the equation. At issue were some NBC broadcasts linking Newton's interests in a Las Vegas casino with organized crime. Richard B. Wirthlin, a well-known and well-respected pollster, was commissioned by Newton's attorneys to document damage to their client's reputation occurring as a result of the NBC broadcasts. His testimony was recorded in 135 pages of trial transcript.[47] For example:

Wirthlin: 36% mentioned that the thing that they had heard negative was that Wayne Newton was associated with organized crime, and 14% mentioned the connection between organized crime and the purchase of a casino.

Newton's Attorney: Would you translate those percentages in terms of numbers of American people?

Wirthlin: Well, that represents about 9½% of our total population.

***

NBC Attorney: So you mean more than half of the people who say, yes, I've heard something negative about him, still say, well, it's an excellent way to describe him to say he's a talented performer?

Wirthlin: . . . You're right.

***

NBC Attorney: But when you ask the question in its most neutral sense or in the most neutral form, what is it that you like the least about Wayne Newton, if you turn to page seven, I think that summarizes the results, it reads as follows: While his singing was the most frequently mentioned positive impression people have about Wayne Newton, it was also cited by 14% of the respondents as what they like least about him.

Wirthlin: That is right.

NBC Attorney: Was that the highest number?

Wirthlin: That is correct.

NBC Attorney: So when you asked people what they liked least about Wayne Newton more people say his singing than anything else?

Wirthlin: That is correct.

NBC Attorney: More people say his singing than say organized crime?

Wirthlin: That is correct.

NBC Attorney: And then it continues, other negative comments were made about Mr. Newton's appearance, his clothes, that was 4% right?

Wirthlin: Correct.

NBC Attorney: And, again, that's higher than the number of people of what they said they liked least about Wayne Newton is his ties to organized crime. And then next after that, or the same level, his hair and his mustache, that was also 4%; is that right?

Wirthlin: Right.

NBC Attorney: So when you ask people in the most neutral way possible what do you like least about Wayne Newton, 14% said the singing, 4% said his appearance, his clothes, another 4% said his hair and his mustache, and you have to go all the way down to 1.6% before you get mafia connections; isn't that right?

Wirthlin: No. You said in the most neutral way . . .

Despite the defense contention that Newton's popularity could be traced more to his mustache, dress, and singing than to alleged connections with organized crime, the jury awarded the singer $19 million in damages. The judge ultimately reduced the figure to just over $5 million. Does the damage award make sense in light of the evidence? The question cannot be answered without first providing the questions the jurors were asked to consider. The trial judge, focusing on the element of defamation, instructed the jury that to find for Newton there must have been proof that:

Mr. Newton was damaged as a direct result of the broadcast of the impression or statement about him. Plaintiff must first prove by a preponderance of the credible evidence that one or more broadcasts he complains about defamed him. A broadcast is defamatory if it appreciably injures his reputation. In deliberating whether plaintiff has met the burden of proving defamation, you must not give any consideration to whether he suffered annoyance, embarrassment or discomfort as a result of the statements he complains about. His own reaction has no bearing upon his reputation.

When I instruct you that a defamatory broadcast is one which appreciably injures reputation, I mean a broadcast which tends to expose to public contempt, ridicule, aversion or disgrace, to make him shunned or avoided or deprived of the friendly association of a considerable number of reputable members of the community. Not every unpleasant or uncomplimentary statement is defamatory. To be defamatory, a statement must tend to bring plaintiff into disrepute, accuse him of a crime, or must prejudice the plaintiff in the eyes of a substantial part of the community.[48]

The jury instructions seem to indicate that Newton must suffer identifiable damage to his reputation. Personal embarrassment, for example, is insufficient. Yet the key may be the requirement that the words "tend" to bring plaintiff into disrepute. This suggests not that the specific words must be proven to *have caused* damage, but that such words *would tend* to cause damage — much as the bad tendency test was applied to political speech in the World War I sedition prosecutions. Note the conceptual difference in law between the need to prove that damage has actually occurred and the less burdensome requirement for proof that certain words would *tend* to cause damage. Note also that while communication science requires rigorous proof and testing before a finding of *tendency* can be put forth, the legal operationalization of tendency requires only that the jury accept intuitive or circumstantial "proof."[49]

Some observations about Newton's trial and use of a public opinion survey are in order.

The survey does not reach the communication science threshold question of whether reputation was damaged, or even the lesser question of whether broadcasts such as NBC's would tend to damage a reputation, at least in terms of communication science. The law does not require such.

The Wirthlin public opinion study is de novo research. And while it is intended for presentation to a jury, it is not jury refereed within the context of scientific rigor. Unlike survey research utilized in theory development, the Newton survey was commissioned for use in litigation. The interpretation of the data was conducted not in the relatively neutral atmosphere of the academy where communication scientists attempt to reduce value laden inferences to a minimum, but in an advocacy-based courtroom. Whatever the potential of the reliability and validity of the data it is important to recognize who was carrying on the interpretation and for what motive.

How important, then, was the survey? In terms of law, the court does not base a decision on the results of the survey per se. Whether or not Newton was defamed in a manner that would carry the tendency to damage his reputation was a question for the jury, and the survey was only one element of the evidence presented. Nonetheless, for whatever motives, attorneys are beginning to recognize the value of communication research and the need to focus on the inherent communication question in any libel case—does a particular message sent through a particular channel damage a particular reputation?

Newton's attorney, Morton Galane, added a new twist to the use of communication research, this time in post-trial proceedings. A second public opinion survey was commissioned. This time the poll looked for a correlation between the reporting of high libel awards and repair of damaged reputation. Galane says the survey "confirmed that the public believes that the reporting of a high libel award in favor of Mr. Newton would be perceived by others as restoration of a positive public image. In short, public vindication is now ongoing."[50]

Galane's interpretation of the data no doubt is intended to serve the needs of plaintiff's attorney. Such advocacy is his job. Nonetheless, it suggests an important area of inquiry for communication researchers. If a reputation has been wrongfully damaged, what palliatives are available? The equation of large awards to reparation of damaged reputation also raises new questions about the function of libel trials and their corresponding damage awards. Note that Galane did *not* say that large awards lead the public to discard already-formed opinions in favor of more positive ones. Rather, he said that *others* will *believe* that *others* will *perceive* that high awards will carry a particular meaning for the public. Questions dealing with perceptions and media are especially well-suited for study by communication researchers. Two studies aimed directly at the question of how people perceive others who have been exposed to defamatory messages are examined below. The notion of perceptions about the effects of media on others is a recognized phenomenon in communication and in psychology.

A final word on the first survey and the trial itself: Based on the judge's instructions with their reliance on a nonscientific concept of the *tendency* to harm, we might question whether the jury is basing judgment on real harm to reputation or on its own theory of how people react to defamatory communication. Moreover, as we indicated earlier, the fault issue, at least intuitively, provides few obvious questions for the communication theorist. Such questions, however, are indeed present and begin to surface when the arena is shifted from the courtroom to the social laboratory.

Third-Person Effects

A research group at the Stanford Institute for Communication Research began a series of experiments in 1987 focusing on the relationship between defamatory communication and reputation. An experiment was designed to investigate the third-person effect within the context of libelous newspaper reports.[51]

The third-person effect was suggested by communication sociologist Phil Davison in 1983.[52] It hypothesizes that: (1) people exposed to media messages will believe that *they* are not as strongly affected by those messages as are *others*; and (2) that people will base their own actions on their perceptions that others are more strongly affected by media messages than they are.

The intent of the Stanford experiment was not only to measure opinion effects, but "to examine readers' judgments of the effect that defamatory news reports had upon themselves, and their perceptions of the effects these reports would have on others."[53] Underlying the concern with third-person effects was the basic question: Do libel juries accurately judge the amount of damage to reputation a given communication will cause? If the third-person hypothesis is operative in jury deliberations, then it is possible that juries overestimate the degree to which reputations are affected by defamatory media reports.

Subjects were randomly assigned to read defamatory and neutral articles in newspapers that were identifiably biased positively or negatively or were neutral toward the defamed news subjects.

Three major conclusions were drawn.

First, subjects perceived defamatory communications as having a stronger effect on others than on themselves.

Next, the perceived effect on others increased as the distance between "other" and "self" increased—subjects perceived that other students are more affected than self; people in the county are more affected than students on campus; people in the state are more affected by the reports than people in the county. Further experiments are underway that focus on this phenomenon, which is called "social distancing theory."

Third, the more the source of the defamatory communication is perceived as negatively biased, the greater the discrepancy between perceived media influence on self and on others. Relative to the other conditions, there is less actual and perceived opinion change in the negatively biased condition, but a greater estimation of communication effect on others.

The study's third finding raises an interesting issue with regard to the constitutional fault requirement. Remember that the legal fault element is intended not to focus on reputation or damage, but to provide a safeguard for the free flow of information. Yet, the study concludes,

> the emphasis at libel trials given to establishing harmful intent on the part of the defendant may intensify jurors' perceptions of a source's negative bias. Such an increase in the perception of source bias would heighten the third person effect and thus heighten the jury's perception that the plaintiff's reputation was damaged. Evidence about the intentions of the source, intended to bear on the fault element in a libel trial, may contribute to the perception of harm.[54]

The fault element, then, with its emphasis on showings of negligence and reckless disregard for the truth may actually encourage large jury awards against the press rather than adding Justice William Brennan's metaphorical "breathing space." Note that this possibility comes to light only when libel is examined from the perspective of communication theory and an experimental social science methodology.

The experiment does not mean that juries actually overestimate the damage done by defamatory news reports. It does, however, provide the first empirical testing aimed specifically at defamatory communication, and it certainly raises the possibility of a vast gulf between the damage juries think defamatory articles cause and the damage they actually cause. The Stanford study is an example of an interdisciplinary approach that goes beyond reasoning that:

Communication theory says X about defamatory reports;

Law says Y about defamatory reports;

Therefore, law is wrong about defamatory reports and should be revised.

Two things distinguish the Stanford approach. First, the study was operationalized taking into account both the rigorous requirements of social science methodology and the actual application and function of law. And second, the study recognized that its goal was not immediate legal reform, but the testing of legal and communication theory.

Journalism professor Albert Gunther conducted a follow-up study at the University of Minnesota intended not only to document the existence of a third-person effect, but to also focus on reader actions related to that effect.[55] Again conducting experiments using defamatory news articles, Gunther examined source credibility and level of judgment factors. Gunther's innovative approach again found a significant third-person effect among subjects exposed to defamatory news articles. Taking his subjects the next step, he asked them to award damages. His findings suggest a profitable line of research. His subjects' decisions to award damages were not related directly to their estimates of the consequences of the defamatory articles. Rather, the damage awards appeared to take into account the newspaper's motivation for publishing the story. Here again, the researcher's intent was not immediate policy reform. Gunther's study identifies communication assumptions embedded in law and empirically tests those assumptions in a controlled setting. His study adds to the literature of communication theory and raises important questions about communication assumptions in law above the level of mere rhetoric.

Fact/Opinion

In a second Stanford study on libel, this time on the fact/opinion distinction, an experimental design was again brought to bear on questions involving law.[56] The First Amendment provides absolute protection in libel law for all statements of opinion, no matter how vitriolic. As a result, the courts have attempted to develop judicial tests to distinguish fact from opinion. As with reputation, there are questions of law here based on assumptions about the ways people perceive and act upon various types of communication.

The experiment tested two possible criteria for such distinctions. The first, page environment of the information (editorial page versus news page of a newspaper), was taken from the four-part test developed in *Ollman v. Evans* (1984).[57] The second, the presence or absence of a by-line, was suggested by earlier survey research that found a significant link between by-line and reader belief that an article was opinion in nature. The experiment also examined the differential effect of perception of fact versus opinion on reader assessment of the defamed person. Do reports perceived as opinion generate negative reputational change to the same degree as reports perceived as factual?

The study found that page environment did influence subjects' perceptions of whether an article was fact or opinion, a finding in keeping with the *Ollman* test's assumption that people recognize the function of the op-ed page. The findings contradicted earlier survey data suggesting by-line as an important reader cue. And, perhaps especially interesting in terms of theories of freedom of expression, the findings suggest that reports perceived as opinion could deliver at least as powerful a reputational sting as reports perceived as factual.

Questioning Assumptions

The available research tells us a good deal about libel. We know that the tort involves concepts of *self* and of reputation, a notion that ties self to *others*. We know there is a tension between constitutional requirements for an uninhibited flow of ideas and common law that represents a consensus of sorts that libel should be prosecuted. We know that assumptions about communication embedded in law are questionable, but that the law is not based on scientific methodology. We have examined a number of approaches to libel, some rooted in law and others in communication.

The function of this chapter is to demonstrate by example the plethora of possibilities for communication research involving libel and to emphasize the point that each has a differing function. Our examples are far from exhaustive. This chapter is also intended to emphasize the necessity for interdisciplinary integrity — that is, the need to recognize that simply because we study libel as communication researchers we cannot ignore the laws and methodological requirements of the legal *system*.

Communication and law raises several questions about libel. How accurate are our perceptions of the amount of damage a defamatory article can do? How accurate are our perceptions of the effects of large libel judgments on reputations? What are the functions of libel awards — are they tools to repair reputations or payments to compensate for damage? Should we balance the risk of harm to the individual against constitutional commands for absolute protection with greater attention to communication science? Or to original intent?

We have not answered these questions. Yet we have provided a rudimentary sense that if we are to attempt to answer such questions at all — for that matter, even to identify appropriate and useful questions — we need to continue to develop an integrated communication and law approach. It is unsettling that we know so little about a tort so common as libel.

NOTES

1. New York Times v. Sullivan, 376 U.S. 254 (1964).
2. Westmoreland v. CBS, 770 F.2d 1168 (D.C. Cir. 1985).

3. Burnett v. National Enquirer, 1444 Cal. App. 3rd 991, Cal. Rptr. 206 (1983).

4. See generally William Prosser and W. Page Keeton, *Law of Torts*, 5th ed. (St. Paul, Minn., 1984); Robert Sack, *Libel, Slander and Related Problems* (New York, 1980).

5. Harry Kalven, Jr., *A Worthy Tradition* (New York, 1988): 60.

6. Alexander Meiklejohn, *Political Freedom* (New York, 1948); "The First Amendment is Absolute," in Philip B. Kurland, ed., *Free Speech and Association* (Chicago, 1975): 1.

7. Schenck v. United States, 249 U.S. 47 (1919); Abrams v. U.S. 250 U.S. 616; see generally Zechariah Chafee, *Free Speech in the United States* (Cambridge, Mass., 1941); Jeremy Cohen, *Congress Shall Make No Law* (Ames, Ia., 1989); Richard Polenberg, *Fighting Faiths* (New York, 1987); Debs v. United States, 249 U.S. 211 (1919).

8. Harry Kalven, Jr., "The New York Times Case: A Note on the Central Meaning of the First Amendment," in Kurland, ed., *Free Speech and Association*, 113–14.

9. See generally Charles A. Miller, *The Supreme Court and the Uses of History* (Cambridge, Mass., 1969); Paul L. Murphy, "Time to Reclaim: The Current Challenge of American Constitutional History," *American Historical Review* 69 (1963).

10. Leonard W. Levy, *Original Intent and the Framers' Constitution* (New York, 1988): 300.

11. Kalven, "The New York Times Case," 85.

12. *Black's Law Dictionary*, 5th ed. (St. Paul, Minn., 1979): 1335.

13. Ronald Farrar, "News Councils and Libel Actions," *Journalism Quarterly* 63 (1986): 509.

14. James Bow and Ben Silver, "Effects of Herbert v. Lando on Small Newspapers and TV Stations," *Journalism Quarterly* 61 (1984): 414.

15. David Anderson, "Presumed Harm: An Item for the Unfinished Agenda of Times v. Sullivan," *Journalism Quarterly* 62 (1985): 24.

16. Ibid., 30.

17. Ibid.

18. Robert Drechsel, "Mass Media Liability for Intentional Infliction of Emotional Distress," *Journalism Quarterly* 289 (1985): 95; "Media Tort Liability for Physical Harm," *Journalism Quarterly* 64 (1987): 99.

19. Ibid., 99.

20. Ibid., 177.

21. Ruth Walden and Emile Netzhammer, "False Light Invasion of Privacy: Untangling the Web of Uncertainty," *Hastings Journal of Communication and Entertainment Law* 9 (1987): 347.

22. Marc Franklin, "Winners, Losers and Why: A Study of Defamation Litigation," *American Bar Foundation Research Journal* (1980): 455; "Suing Media for

Libel: A Litigation Study," *American Bar Foundation Research Journal* (1981): 797.

23. Franklin, "Winners, Losers and Why," 499.

24. Ibid., 500.

25. F. Dennis Hale, "The Federalization of Libel by Two Supreme Courts," paper presented to the Association for Education in Journalism and Mass Communication (1988); see also "Freedom of Expression: The Warren and Burger Courts," *Communications and the Law* 9 (1987): 3.

26. Hale, "The Federalization of Libel," 32.

27. David Anderson, "Media Success in the Supreme Court," Gannett Center for Media Studies Working Paper (1987).

28. Ibid., 13.

29. Linda Lawson, "Trial by Jury: Problems with Jury Instructions in Libel Cases," paper presented to Western Communications Educators' Conference (1985).

30. Jerome H. Skolnick, "Foreword: The Sociological Tort of Defamation," *California Law Review* 74 (1986): 677.

31. Ibid.

32. Robert C. Post, "The Social Foundations of Defamation Law: Reputation and the Constitution," *California Law Review* 74 (1986): 691, 741.

33. Ibid., 741.

34. Robert N. Bellah, "The Meaning of Reputation in American Society," *California Law Review* 74 (1986): 743.

35. Randall P. Bezanson, Gilbert Cranberg, and John Soloski, *Libel Law and the Press* (New York, 1987).

36. Randall P. Bezanson, "Libel Law and the Press: Setting the Record Straight," *Iowa Law Review* 71 (1985): 226.

37. Ibid.

38. Ibid., 228.

39. David Pritchard, "What People Do When They Don't Like What the Press Says About Them: An Exploratory Study of Libel as a Social Construct." Paper presented to the Association for Education in Journalism and Mass Communication (1987).

40. Everette E. Dennis and Eli M. Noam, eds., *The Cost of Libel* (New York, 1987).

41. Ronald Farrar, "News Councils and Libel Actions," *Journalism Quarterly* 63 (1986): 509.

42. "A Proposal for the Reform of Libel Law: The Report of the Libel Reform Project of the Annenberg Washington Program" (Washington, D.C., 1988).

43. See generally John Monohan and Laurens Walter, *Social Science in Law: Cases and Materials* (Mineola, N.Y., 1985); Kenneth Culp Davis, "Facts in Lawmaking," *Columbia Law Review* 80 (1980): 931.

44. Suzanne Bonamici, "The Use and Reliability of Survey Evidence in Deceptive Advertising Cases," *Oregon Law Review* 62 (1983): 561.

45. See generally Monohan and Walker, *Social Science in Law*.

46. See generally Don R. Pember, *Mass Media Law* (Dubuque, Ia., 1987); Prosser and Keeton, *Law of Torts*. The relation of the tort elements to the separate concerns of reputation and freedom of expression are discussed in Jeremy Cohen and Albert Gunther, "Libel as Communication Phenomena," *Communications and the Law* 9 (October 1987): 9.

47. "Reporter's Transcript of the Proceedings Before the Honorable M.D. Crocker," Jury trial (19 November 1986).

48. Reported in *Libel Litigation 1988* (New York, 1988): 732–3.

49. For a general discussion of the use of survey evidence in libel trials, see Jeremy Cohen and Sara Spears, "Newtonian Communication: Shaking the Libel Tree for Empirical Damages," *Journalism Quarterly* (forthcoming).

50. "News Notes: Newton Accepts Reduced Damages Award," 15 *Media Law Reporter* 42 (1989).

51. Jeremy Cohen, Diana Mutz, Vincent Price, and Albert Gunther, "Perceived Impact of Defamation: An Experiment on Third Person Effects," *Public Opinion Quarterly* 52 (1988): 161.

52. W. Phillips Davison, "The Third-Person Effect in Communication," *Public Opinion Quarterly* 47 (1983): 1.

53. Cohen, Mutz, Price, and Gunther, "Perceived Impact of Defamation," 165.

54. Ibid., 173.

55. Albert Gunther, "What We Think Others Think: The Role of Cause and Consequence in the Third Person Effect," paper presented to the International Communication Association (1989).

56. Jeremy Cohen, Diana Mutz, Clifford Nass, and Laurie Mason, "Experimental Test of Some Notions of the Fact/Opinion Distinction in Libel," *Journalism Quarterly* 66 (1989): 11.

57. Ollman v. Evans 750F. 2d 970 (1984); see generally Timothy Gleason, "The Fact/Opinion Distinction in Libel Law," *Hastings Journal of Communication and Entertainment Law* 10 (1988): 763.

5

RECONCILING COMMUNICATION WITH LAW

How can scholars successfully apply the rules of communication research to law when the rules of law and communication research were developed to fulfill differing functions? A unified approach requires fidelity both to the philosophy of social research and to the advocacy-based structure of result-oriented jurisprudence.

Previous chapters have explored some of the concepts and theories of law and of freedom of expression. It is clear that those interested in law, legal scholarship, and communication share a number of interests. It is also clear that while there is overlap in the ways researchers in each discipline approach their work, methodological and conceptual differences are prevalent and pivotal.

We have seen that the traditional building blocks of legal theory and of theories of freedom of expression can be found in the qualitative research methodologies of case law analysis and historiography. Focusing on libel we also have examined the potential to use social science in general, and communication science in particular, to further our understanding of communication and law. This chapter continues the focus on communication as it continues to sketch a conceptual map of the intersection between communication and law.

A scholar interested in communication and law faces numerous obstacles to the pursuit of productive research because of the nature of the undertaking. Not least of all, little research within the discipline *communication and law* has been attempted, leaving a dearth of useful maps to follow. Even more difficult, perhaps, is the interdisciplinary nature of the field. Prodigious amounts of disciplined, scholarly preparation are required both in law and in communication. Unfortunately, most scholars specialize in one *or* the other. As a result researchers are easy prey to the trap of making assumptions either about law or about communication that place them on a false trail. We need to recognize the hazards in order to avoid them.

This chapter begins with a landscape of ruts and stumps cluttering the research path. They comprise nothing like an exhaustive list. Taken as a whole, however, they point to a unified problem: the difficulty of maintaining validity across disciplines in an interdisciplinary approach. How can scholars successfully apply the rules of communication research to law when the rules for law and communication research were developed to fulfill differing functions?

With this as a foundation, the chapter examines social science and communication research principles that may be very familiar to those trained in quantitative methods, but less so for those schooled in traditional legal approaches.

Values and the potential for bias in research require special consideration in a scholarly process that integrates the value laden norms of legal studies and advocacy-based legal procedures with the social science objective of unbiased objectivity. As with theoretical and methodological characteristics distinctive of one discipline or another, value considerations between disciplines also must be accounted for. The chapter closes with a consideration of the role of values in communication and law.

Our search for safe passage begins with a conceptual map of our most important landmark: communication.

CONCEPTIONAL, DEFINITIONAL, AND THEORETICAL HAZARDS

Communication Carries Multiple Meanings

What do we mean when our reference to *communication* is to a scholarly discipline rather than to industries such as publishing, film making, and advertising? The question is basic, but it is neither elementary nor uncomplicated. Universities continue to cut across traditional disciplinary boundaries between speech and rhetoric, journalism, telecommunications, film, mass media studies, communication science, and even library science with aggregated structural components in departments and schools of communication(s) that are more the result of historical accident and political machination than pedagogy.

It's no wonder that there is confusion over just what communication is. Ph.D. communication students at one university study scientific method and social science theory exclusively. At another, there is no requirement for quantitative course work. Doctoral candidates there must concentrate on institutional or historical, legal, or critical approaches devoid of what has come to be known as the quantitative approach. Nonetheless, at the end of the dissertation defense, each will hold an advanced degree in communication.[1] Adding to this stew are a growing number of communication professors who hold their advanced degrees not in communication, but in sociology, American studies, history, and law. And of course there are many universities without communication programs where the study of communication topics are undertaken in departments of political science, English, and anthropology.

Communication science. The *Handbook of Communication Science* distinguishes scientific from other communication approaches. Communication researchers Steven Chaffee and Charles Berger write:

> Communications science seeks to understand the production, processing, and effects of symbol and signal systems by developing testable theories, containing lawful generalizations, that explain phenomena associated with production, processing, and effects.

***

> Most scholars in the discipline should see a relatively close fit between their research and the view our definition advances. But we also have colleagues engaged in communication inquiry whose research activities *cannot* be subsumed under our definition. Individuals who criticize the symbolic output of individuals or the media, for example, are not doing communication *science.* Those involved in these critical efforts ordinarily employ a set of idealized esthetic standards that are not derived from any scientific theory. Researchers whose job it is to make ethical or moral judgments about the communicative conduct of persons or institutions are not communication scientists by our definition. Neither are reformists who seek to change public policies concerning communication institutions, even when they gather social scientific data to support their arguments. Finally, there are analysts who seek to explain individual communication events in their own terms, without recourse to broader theoretical principles; we would not classify their work, valuable though it often is, as communication science.

***

> The key issue here is that science seeks to explain by developing general principles that can be used to account for specific events or classes of events.[2]

Functions and goals. Not everything that communication researchers do falls under the heading of communication science. Nor should it. For those interested in communication and law a number of approaches are

· productive. Whatever the approach, there are two recurring first level questions for scholars conducting social research in communication and law:

1) What are the goals of the research — that is, what is it that we hope to learn; and
2) What is the function of the research design — that is, what *can* the type of research contemplated tell us?

Suppose, for example, the question before us is whether the presence of television cameras in an appellate courtroom during arguments by counsel will affect due process. We may want to borrow some interviewing and observation tools from journalists, some measurement and evaluation tools from social scientists, and some established norms from legal scholars. The goal of the research is to determine whether the presence of cameras in the courtroom makes a qualitative difference to the process and to the end product. The function of the research is not communication or even legal theory. It is simply whether the variable of electronic news gathering equipment makes an important difference, and we can reach a very useful conclusion without theory. Our question boils down to one of policy. Even without a theoretical base, however, few would argue that our interest is strictly rooted in law. Our approach clearly is a branch of communication studies.

We need not generate scientific theory to proclaim ourselves members of the communication research community. Biographies of jurists such as Hugo Black or William Douglas or William Brennan — individuals whose opinions and dissents on the Supreme Court have done much to shape the law of communication — provide valuable insight into freedom of expression, which as we have noted earlier includes both law and communication. History is not communication science, but it is an element of communication studies. Scholars from Critical Legal Studies also add to our insight, but again outside the scientific definition advanced by Berger and Chaffee.

Historiography. In fact, little disciplinary confusion arises where historians and other nonscientists have examined phenomena involving both communication and law. Cornell University professor Richard Polenberg, for example, produced an important history of *U.S. v. Abrams* (1919) in his 1987 publication of *Fighting Faiths.*[3] Using the research strategies of the historian, Polenberg probed the Supreme Court's opinion and Oliver Wendell Holmes' dissent — his first sympathetic vote for freedom of expression. Polenberg also documented the social and political forces that led to passage and enforcement of the 1917 Espionage Act and its 1918 Sedition Amendment, the statute upon which *Abrams* was prosecuted. He followed Abrams and his defendant colleagues through a trial in which Judge Henry Delamar Clayton, Jr., repeatedly implied to the jury the defendants' guilt. Referring to their early-dawn distribution of Socialist leaflets opposing the United States expeditionary forces in Russia, Clayton told the jury that when we "do things that we are not ashamed of, and we are not violating the law . . . we come out in the open, but when we do things questionable, that is the time when other methods are resorted to, and I am going to leave it to the jury to determine whether the intention is honest or not."[4]

The text is dramatic: vermin in the jail cells; claims of prisoners beaten and locked in cubicles so small they could not turn; and deportation from the United States to Russia in which Abrams and his friends were made to bear the cost of their forced exodus.

Does Polenberg's extralegal detail help us to understand better either law or communication or, for that matter, qualify as the study of either? Holmes in his well-known address, "The Path of the Law," pointed out the folly of such detail for the attorney:

> The attorney's job [involves] eliminating . . . all the dramatic elements with which his client's story has clothed it, and retaining only the facts of legal import, up to the final analysis and abstract universals of theoretic jurisprudence. The reason why a lawyer does not mention that his client wore a white hat when he made a contract, while Mrs. Quickly would be sure to dwell upon it along with the partial gilt goblet and the sea-coal fire, is that he foresees that the public force will act the same way whatever his client had upon his head.[5]

But we are not acting as attorneys for clients, and Polenberg's detail is not intended to set courtroom strategy. In the narrowest sense, it is not the study of law. Nor does Polenberg's history of the repression of freedom of expression function as communication theory. Yet the broad strokes from Professor Polenberg's brush provide context and insight that undoubtedly are an integral element of communication studies that helps us to understand the law as it involves communication, but not communication itself.

Other examples could be drawn and applied for the cases of Critical Legal Studies, research in media case law, and for policy research under the communications studies umbrella. These cross-disciplinary approaches are not confusing as long as the researcher and the reader bear in mind function: What is the function of the history of freedom of expression? What is the function of policy research?

Communication studies. Our purpose is neither to exclude, nor to accept definitions so large that they are useless. Rather, we require an organizational and definitional scheme that allows us to share meaning without dismissing the importance of colleagues whose work differs in function and form from our own.

In the most general sense, many of us work in *communication studies* — a generic that accommodates communication scientists as well as critical analysts, historians, policy analysts, and media law scholars. Whether we are interested in the application of libel law to broadcast journalism, or reader abilities to distinguish between fact and opinion in defamatory newspaper articles, or the judicial voting patterns of justices broken down by political affiliation, our interest in law has roots in communication and our research in some way involves communication.

The mixture is clouded when we enter the realm of theory. Are we attempting to develop communication theory? legal theory? A theory of freedom of expression? For the communication scientist working with freedom of expression a reasonable goal is the productive use of communication theory to explain or to generate new legal theory. Communication studies includes many approaches. *Communication and law* denotes an integration of communication and legal theory as an ultimate goal.

Does this mean that we in fact are establishing a hierarchy among research types? The answer is yes and no. Again, many types of research are productive. In that sense, no: There is no hierarchy.

It is also important to recognize, however, that the mission of the communication scholar is to generate knowledge about communication. Scholars may do this through historical research. They may do this through the development of critical theory. The hierarchy then is addressed not so much at the distinctions among research methodologies as at purpose. Does the research advance knowledge and understanding of communication? Does it integrate communication and law?

When we talk about communication, then, or about social research in communication, we really are talking about many different things. Communication science strives for theory and utilizes scientific reasoning and method. Communication studies include communication science, historiography, institutional and individual criticism, and case law where they involve some aspect of communications. For the communication researcher, the hierarchy places the search for communication theory and the appropriate use of communication theory in communication and law at the top rung. A sense of direction and of the value of communication research is maintained as long as the issue of function — what the research is intended for — is considered openly and early.

Law Is Not Science

It should be clear by now that law and science have differing functions that make their integration difficult. Yet one premise of this text is that integration not only is possible, but that communication science may play an important role in the development of legal theory.

A 1927 presentation to the Association of American Law Schools by philosopher Morris Cohen focused on issues such as the use of science in law and on law as a science. Cohen lamented what he saw as university law schools abdicating their responsibility to go beyond the very practical venture of training lawyers. The job of the university was theory, and Cohen championed the need to "introduce theoretic studies as remote from immediately practical legal issues as are pathology in the school of medicine, physiological psychology in the school of education, or rational mechanics in the school of engineering."[6]

LAW AND SCIENTIFIC METHOD
Morris Cohen

If scientific method be a way of avoiding certain human pitfalls in the search for truth, then the law surely compares favorably in this respect with other human occupations. Court procedure to determine whether A and B did make a contract, or whether C did commit a criminal act, shows a regard for orderly attainment of truth that compares very favorably with the procedure of a vestry board in determining the fitness of a minister, or of a college in selecting a professor.

When we come, however, to the appellate work of higher courts, in which new public policies are decided under the guise of their legality or constitutionality, we find courts making all sorts of factual generalizations without adequate information . . . Yet the law cannot simply and uncritically accept all the opinions of economists and sociologists. After all, on many important points social scientists are not agreed among themselves.[7] [Published by permission of Transaction Publishers, from *Law and the Social Order*, by Morris R. Cohen. Copyright © 1982 by Transaction Publishers.]

Questions such as those Morris Cohen raises as to whether social science can provide "truth" for the courts have received a good deal of discussion during the 20th century, and there is renewed discussion as technical issues involving everything from gene splicing to artificial intelligence crowd the dockets. There is another aspect to the difference between science and law that goes beyond the practical issues of whether the courts are equipped to deal with scientific revolutions, or whether the academy should devote resources to theoretical pursuits, perhaps at the cost of short-term practical needs.

"Whatever services scientific method is to render," Cohen said, " it is reasonable to demand that it shall not hinder the growth of the science to which it ministers."[8] Law is not lame without social science. And while debates continue over the *truth* to be found in positivism, natural law, purposive jurisprudence, and other schools of judicial decision making, a central fact remains constant. Law seeks to provide a set of rules that are, whether moral or not, whether based on scientific truth or not, enforceable. In essence, law is social policy. If, then, a communication researcher can offer to a court the scientific truth that the presence of cameras will not alter the outcome of an appellate court session, it makes absolutely no difference that the rule the court follows is one barring cameras. Furthermore, the scholar studying the court's ruling will gain little "legal perspective" by stopping to consider the possible effects the presence of cameras have on judicial functions.

The relation of law to science, then, raises three questions:

1) Can science provide the law with help in ascertaining the facts about physical, behavioral, or psychological phenomena? Yes. Scientific method can be used to discover or document social facts.

2) Can courts make good use of scientific data? Under some circumstances, yes. There may be times when the cost in time or in resources makes scientific data undesirable. There may be times when the uncertainty of scientific data provides limited benefit. There may be times when the courts are not equipped to understand the esoteric presentations of the sciences. These, however, are caveats that must be considered on a case-by-case basis. They are not impenetrable barriers. In general, courts can and do make use of scientific data through expert testimony or by judicial notice.

3) Can law, then, take full advantage of scientific method and adopt for itself a scientific approach? Here the answer is no. Judges must provide legal justifications for their decisions. These justifications, which are explana-

tions of legal reasoning, must rely primarily not on scientific truth but on the continuation through consistent decision making a system that conforms to legislatively drawn rules, tradition, or constitutional commands. The enforcement of that law — at least in a democracy — is not found in nature but in (a) the force of the state, and (b) the legitimacy of the courts generated and nourished by judicial ability to stay within the confines of what is perceived of as fair and right, or of what the public will tolerate, or of what the State will condone and uphold. A judicial decision — even one involving empirically testable assumptions of fact — is not beholden to scientific truth, but to the truth of a system of laws perpetuated by subservience, either forced or by consent, to that very system. At best, science can advance legal theory and aid in the ascertainment of fact. At worst, science may cloud legal reasoning.

Legal Theory Is Not the Same as Scientific Theory

When we talk about a "theory of law," we may be referring to any number of things. It may be an established set of juristic principles that govern trial or appellate decision making. Theory instead may refer to more global issues such as the relations among law, authority, and legitimacy. Or legal theory may focus on distinctions between laws and rights, privileges and principles.

Attention to these theoretical approaches is far beyond the scope of this discussion — although familiarity with legal philosophers, theoreticians, and historians such as Morris Cohen, Ronald Dworkin, H.L.A. Hart, Carl Joachim Friedrich, and others can only aid the communication and law scholar seeking the benefit of dialogue rather than the challenge of reinventing the wheel.[9] The basic requirement for the communication and law scholar is to understand that legal theory seeks to provide rules or laws that will accomplish identifiable objectives. The theory may be based on incentive or disincentive. It may be tolerant or not. It may recognize natural law or common law or divine law.

Legal theory may benefit from knowledge of, and the perspective provided by, communication research. In the end, however, the function of communication theory is to understand communication phenomena. The function of legal theory is not necessarily to understand a process or to discover a physical or psychological truth, but to govern by creating a process. Communication research seeks to understand processes that govern rather than to create a governing process.

The Study of Law Involving Communication Is Not Necessarily the Study of Communication

Legal research, even when it focuses on the press, advertising, telecommunication, public relations, and intellectual property is not in and of itself the study of communication. A 1988 Supreme Court ruling, for example, barred demonstrators from picketing outside the private home of a physician. The Wisconsin physician performed legal abortions. An anti-abortion group stationed members outside his house, usually quietly, but sometimes resorting to slogan shouting and on occasion telling neighbors that the "doctor kills babies." A local ordinance banned the pickets.

The Court's 6–3 majority opinion in *Frisby v. Schultz* (1987) framed the issue as one pitting privacy against freedom of expression.[10] While demonstrators may march past a house, privacy rights may subordinate expression when there is picketing "focused on, and taking place in front of a particular residence," the Court said.

Examining the judicial handling of the clash between the rights of privacy and free expression tells us about the law. It may even help us to understand one particular channel of communication — picketing an individual house — and how that channel may be blocked without offending the Constitution. In the popular sense it seems to tell us something about communication. We may deduce from the manner in which the law is interpreted and applied that there won't be much communication between the doctor and his detractors, at least in front of his house.

Does the analysis of the Court's opinion really tell us, however, about communication? Does it contribute to a theoretical understanding of the processes and effects of communication or of the relations between communication and law? Does it suggest legal theory informed by real knowledge about communication? Our reading of *Frisby v. Schultz* falls into the category of legal studies and it tells us something about freedom of expression, which in turn qualifies it for inclusion in communication studies. But while the analysis happens to involve communication, it does not involve the *process and effects* of communication or communication theory in a scientific manner, or the sociology of communication, either. To understand relations and thereby generate useful theory we must accommodate those processes and effects. We cannot claim that law should operate in fashion X based on communication as scientific truth without the development of communication theory to back up calls for communication-conscious law each time law impacts upon communication.

Whatever the potential present throughout judicial decisions involving communication, the majority of research appearing in the literature both of law and of communication studies is legal research. It is descriptive analysis of case law. The focus is on judicial decisions and, to a lesser extent, legal theory—especially as case law and theory relate to professional practices and norms.

On occasion the literature expands to include freedom of expression, which we distinguished in a formal sense from law in the preceding chapters. Strictly speaking, however, the only relation between the majority of legal writing *involving* communication and communication as a distinct *discipline* is the fact that the libel suits, prior restraints, sedition prosecutions, advertising regulations, and broadcast rules that led to the cases under review involved communication in the popular sense. Communication occurred as people wrote or spoke words that led to civil or criminal adjudication. There is a dearth of communication studies material that integrates communication theory and law. Inquiry into the application of law rather than research about communication and law remains the norm.

This is not to say that there is no movement among communication researchers on the substantive issues of freedom of expression or *communication and law*. There are researchers responding not as attorneys or journalism teachers advising reporters and students, but as members of a discipline called communication. Even here, however, the water is turbulent and hazardous.

Communication Science Informs Us About Phenomena, Not About Jurisprudence

Current vogue involves the practice of reducing law to a question of communication logic. Is, for example, libel law logical in terms of what we know about human communication and about public reactions to the mass media? Packer applied a communication model to military restrictions on freedom of expression and found that the communication literature does not support the repressive attitudes towards expression found in the Uniform Code of Military Justice.[11] Haskins, Patzke, and Price conducted a general review of speech based upon communication models. They concluded that an "[un]enlightened view of communication . . . predominates both the Court's and society's view."[12] Cohen and Gunther contrasted the legal and communication science views of reputational damage. They concluded, "Behavioral science has not yet been called on to provide and probably cannot yet provide a simple and useful formula for defamation. But that cannot be in and of itself a sufficient excuse for the law to act in this area without knowledge. And without knowledge of the relation between communication and reputation, law and adherence to law must operate contingent upon authority that may well be arbitrary."[13]

The problem with this line of approach — asking communication type questions about the law and using communication theory to critique the law — is not that it is *wrong*. In fact, assumptions about the processes and effects of communication upon which some laws are based do contradict what we know about communication. The application of communication logic to law seems to make sense and so it is seductive.

The sedition legislation of World War I, for example, *appeared* to be based on a belief that words had a powerful and dangerous effect. Public opposition to the draft or the war with Germany or with the Bolshevik Revolution was akin, according to Oliver Wendell Holmes, to "shouting fire in a theater and causing a panic." This effects paradigm, of course, *is* contradicted by what we know about the difficulty of shaping public opinion. The shout of fire in a small, dark room might cause a panic. But it is not in keeping with what we have tested about communication to believe that shouting political rhetoric from a street corner will drive a nation to panic.

If the logic of communication theory appears to challenge a major Supreme Court decision, then why question the usefulness of the approach? Consider approaching the World War I sedition legislation from a context outside of communication science. If we establish variables and phenomena we are interested in as historians or political scientists instead of as communication scientists, we are led away from the emerging folk wisdom: *The law was based on a mistaken belief about communication.* A strong case can be mounted to argue that sedition laws were based not as much on a powerful effects paradigm as on a basic desire to punish the socialists and pacifists and to frighten others from joining them. Despite his opinions for the Court upholding convictions against Schenck and others charged with sedition, Holmes wrote a friend: "Now I hope the President will pardon him and some other poor devils with whom I have more sympathy. Those whose cases have come before us have seemed poor fools whom I should have been inclined to pass over if I could. The greatest bores in the world are the come-outers who are cock-sure of a dozen nostrums. The dogmatism of a little education is hopeless."[14] This does not sound like the writing of a Supreme Court Justice concerned that some soapbox oratory will bring down the walls of the White House.

The *apparent* basis of the sedition law — communication effects and the powerful effects paradigm — is unsound. We know this based on communication science. But we do not know and cannot know from communication science that fear of powerful effects was in fact the basis of the sedition laws. In fact, it is likely that such a belief was at best a small, if useful, element of the overall dynamic. Communication science informs us about phenomena, not about legislative intent or judicial temperament.

There Are Times When Communication Should Be the Secondary Rather Than the Primary Focus

It is tempting to hold the powerful effects paradigm up to laws regulating the press and say, "See. Your law is based on weak thinking. Thinking that ignores science." And from this vantage it is tempting to equate law that assigns predictable and powerful mass media effects with the superstitions of the Dark Ages — a mixture of black magic and absolute authority. Depending on the intended use of the comparison, it may simply be whistling in the wind. The danger is ever present that the powerful effects paradigm provides no more than a straw man to slay — a momentarily fulfilling act that does little to halt the advance of real dragons. (Even in the discipline of communication itself it is popular to attack the powerful effects paradigm — yet as Chaffee and Hochheimer pointed out, there is no evidence to support a claim that any researcher ever actually advanced a bullet or hypodermic needle theory.)[15] The motivation behind the legislation and the jurisprudence that is speech repressive may well be based not on faulty scientific reasoning, however, but on a desire to forward an agenda other than the obvious one — an agenda influenced heavily by the world of *realpolitik*.

The error we make here as communication researchers is to gallop forward with theory we believe to be explanatory without first searching the horizon for at least equally productive explanations. Here social research requires that we be prepared to set communication science aside long enough to consider the research of the communication historian. This does not contradict our instinct that communication science does not back up the effects notion the law appears to embrace. But it does suggest that while our notion may be true, it does little to help us understand the World War I sedition trials. The public cared little about what the effects of speech were. They cared about silencing the minority viewpoint.

To carry the argument forward, the military today may care little about the actual effect of specific speech and a great deal about the relation of unregulated expression and unquestioning discipline in battle. We can hold the military code up to the communication model and chastise the generals for their unenlightened approach to communication science. Yet if our theories are applied to a set of concerns and phenomena different from those considered by tank commanders, submarine captains, flight officers, and infantry sergeants, their validity becomes questionable.

Still, this type of inquiry is not without benefit. Examining law and regulation under the light of communication theory has heuristic value. It is a means of raising useful questions about policy, law, and communication. It is a means to look for relationships among law and communication and freedom of expression. These kinds of conceptual exercises must be undertaken, of course, with the awareness that law often does not seek scientific truth. The truth of law is the stuff of political and social compromise. Libel, access, assembly, and petition arises not from physical and behavioral laws (at least so far as we know without subjecting the possibility to empirical testing) so much as from social compact.

Ignore the communication model? No. But just as the historian must avoid familiarity with late 20th-century ideals and norms in the interpretation of 18th-century motives, communication scholars must take care to use the tool of communication science only for those jobs for which it is appropriate.

When Judges "Say" Communication Effects
They May Not Be "Talking About"
Communication Effects

Our focus as communication researchers studying First World War cases may be further clouded by the language of the Court's opinions. Indeed, the Court does appear to embrace the powerful effects paradigm. The Constitution, Holmes explains in *Schenck*, does not "protect a man from an injunction from uttering words that may have all the effect of force."[16] It sounds as if Holmes is saying that words capable of generating a powerful effect may be censored or punished. The researcher schooled in the Court's jurisprudence, however, will be on the lookout for the difference between what the judiciary writes for legal precedent and public consumption in a published opinion, and the full range of dynamics that comprise judicial decision making. The Court cannot arbitrarily forbid speech. It needs an acceptable justification that will not offend the Constitution, common law, or the public sensibility. These rationalizations, however, are not always the same as the judiciaries' reasons. The Court — any American court for that matter — must justify its decisions in a manner in keeping with boundaries long established. A *duty* to protect the public from a "clear and present danger" caused by powerful communications is well within that boundary. A desire to punish anyone who disagrees with the government is not.

Taking the vantage of the history scholar and the legal scholar in combination, it is not at all out of line to view the World War I trials as political trials. Historian Richard Polenberg's chronicle of the arrest, trial and appeal of Abrams and his colleagues provides convincing evidence. First Amendment scholar Harry Kalven, Jr., calls the Abrams trial "a political trial of Bolsheviks."[17] As communication scientists we want to look at the lack of danger the words of *Schenck* or *Abrams* or *Debs* actually held. This is an especially seductive path to take 70 years after the fact, its curves circumventing the differences over time. The dangers of approaching the first decades of the 20th century schooled in the perceptions of the information age are real. The path that focuses on the clear and present danger or the bad tendency of the communication acts prosecuted tells us little about the law that was.

Our sedition cases cast differing shadows for communication researchers schooled in the methods and substance of law, history, and science. Conclusions, even those that are justified within a narrow context, can easily mislead when they reflect only a single approach. The need for an interdisciplinary approach is nowhere more obvious. The communication model helps us to identify the need to challenge the Court's decisions to uphold sedition convictions. Within communication studies, the discipline of communication science provides the legal scholar with a new context from which to identify important questions. Communication science is no less necessary to the process of inquiry in law if it cannot then be used directly in a courtroom.

A Quantitative Study Is Not Always Communication Research

A communication historian who was more than a little skeptical of quantitative research and its application to his chosen discipline used to tell his seminar students, "Historians capable of thinking do so. Those who can't, count." It seems that we spend a lot of time in communication telling ourselves that the battle between the Chi-Squares and the Qualitative researchers is long buried. Never mind that our scholarly organizations continue to maintain divisions that appear to be based on the lack or presence of numbers in their methodological arsenals rather than on real conceptual differences. We continue to confuse the tool of quantitative methodologies with conceptual and theoretical research, a problem perhaps confounded in communication and law by the small size of our esoteric literature. There are few models to follow and learn from.

Our purpose is not to rank various methodologies or even to suggest that one line of research is more important or more useful than another. In truth, the authors do have a bias — the job of the communication researcher is to develop theory, communication theory capable of driving legal theory in a context that recognizes and respects the interdisciplinary nature of the endeavor.

Toward these goals we need to be aware that even research that uses quantitative methodologies, that involves communication law, and that generates clearly useful information for those interested in communication is not necessarily communication research.

David Anderson, a University of Texas law professor especially well-known in the field of libel law, conducted a study in 1987 as a senior fellow at the Gannett Center for Media Research. He examined Supreme Court cases involving the media. In his introduction to "Media Success in the Supreme Court," Anderson states, "In fact, [the media] have won barely more cases than they have lost. Of 199 cases decided by he Supreme Court through the 1985–86 term (excluding 7 cases with media litigants on both sides), the media have won only 53 percent."[18]

Anderson's careful compilation of data provides a useful summary and a meaningful way to consider the success rate of media litigants. His study has the feel of empiricism in the sense that he systematically collects and categorizes information about observable phenomena — the decisions of the U.S. Supreme Court. And from his observations, Anderson is able to reach useful conclusions that should be of great interest to practitioners and scholars alike. Anderson concludes,

> A litigation strategy based on an assumption that the Supreme Court generally or historically is solicitous of media interests obviously would be misguided: nor can one assume that an unsolicitous Court must be an aberration that will right itself when some new justices are appointed. For media litigants in the Supreme Court, the chief aberration has been the 16 years of the Warren Court. Throughout the rest of its history, the Court has been consistently less favorable to media than to the general run of litigants.[19]

Anderson's study is a study of law. Like others we have examined and will continue to examine it seems to involve communication on some level, but it does *not* tell us about the process and effects of communication. Certainly, Anderson's work provides a major contribution to the general interest area of communication studies. It does so, however, without membership in the *discipline* of *communication*.

Communication Is Social Science: Social Science Is Not Communication

Related to issues involving the use of quantitative or nonquantitative research tools is the distinction between social science and communication. It is in the same vein as the difference between a square and a rectangle in the sense that both a square and a rectangle meet the definitional constructs of a rectangle: a four-sided figure with corners of 90 degrees. A rectangle, however, does not contain the additional requirement that its parallel sides each be of equal length.

If we think of social science as the behavioral and psychological study of human individuals and their relationships, surely communication science is a discipline to be included. The logic of communication science is in fact the logic of social science. The distinction arises in two important ways. Communication asks questions about communication. The variables used by a communication researcher may be quite different from those used by other social scientists whose orientation is in psychology or sociology or political science.

Why is the difference important? Because failure to recognize the distinction between social science and communication directs us away from our primary concern: the generation of communication theory and legal theory cognizant of communication. When we say social science and law, we are including much in that phrase that is not communication. One need only look at academic journals such as *Law and Society* and *Law and Social Inquiry* to see that a great deal of social scientific method and thought is being applied to law — but only rarely are social scientists involved in *communication and law* research.

Ignorance of the Law Is No Excuse

Sometimes a lack of familiarity with the principles and process of law can trip up otherwise well-intentioned researchers schooled in communication but lacking formal training in law. One type of error that has surfaced in published work is the assumption that any case involving freedom of expression in some manner involves the First Amendment. Yet cases such as *Chandler v. Florida* (1981) speak otherwise.[20] The Court ruled in *Chandler* that the presence of cameras in a courtroom does not, in and of itself, provide prima facie evidence of a violation of due process. While the case involved communication and news gathering because television reporters use cameras, no First Amendment issues were raised.

A related error occurs when "communication" type cases are grouped together too loosely. It is obviously useful to examine Supreme Court voting records covering cases involving communication, and a powerful means to accomplish this is to use the statistical tools of the social scientist. At this junction, however, the communication researcher must attend to a key differentiation between communication and law. The law does not group all communication cases as a single type, while it may be tempting for communication to do so. The logic goes like this: Obscenity involves communication, libel involves communication, advertising involves communication, and prior restraint involves communication — how did the Court and its individual members vote on communication cases? Very different judicial standards are applied, however, to fact situations involving obscenity and libel, and prior restraint, and commercial speech. The researcher who operationalizes his study in ways that make sense from a communication studies perspective may miss important distinctions in law. Operationalization must take into account law as well as the research design convenience of the social scientist.

A study about the use of electronic data bases by attorneys provides a third example. Here some students were looking for variables that would predict the likelihood of database use in law offices. Yet because they did not understand law or the practice of law they did not control for the possibility that database use would be higher for some *types* of cases than for others — for example, higher in litigation of appellate cases that involve significant precedent and lower for work involving the drafting of wills, contracts, and other standard procedures.

The students had internal validity in their study, but they lacked the means by which to weigh the importance of their findings because they did not know about the existence of a variable that may or may not have significantly altered their results.

THE ELEMENTS OF RESEARCH

Too often we fail to ask a very basic question before piecing communication theory into the research puzzle. In what ways are our communication logic, or historical, or jurisprudential lines of questioning useful? Are they appropriate to what we want to study? Do they tell us what we think they tell us? The rules of legal inquiry are different from the rules of communication inquiry because we study law and communication for different reasons. Acting without considering basic questions about what we hope to accomplish subjects communication research to questions of validity.

Expectations and Who the
Research Is For

A common question posed to communication scientists by legal scholars is: Why should a court be interested in communication theory? Claims that communication theory doesn't back up legal principle, after all, hardly impact upon the individual fact situations that make up the litigation process. Experimental subjects and mock jurors may be immune to the dangers of prejudicial publicity. But real trials involve 12 individual jurors who may be the exceptions to statistical generalizations. Averages don't work when it comes to individual rights within the legal process. And so the familiar arguments go. Yet statistical data do tell us something about the process. We may want to know, for example, whether some processes lead to inherently unfair culminations. Does jury size make a predictable difference in deliberation outcome? Does exposure to identifiable types of extrajudicial material have a predictable effect on jurors?

Communication research involving law may be categorized using numerous conceptualizations, some orthogonal, some unique. Since we are concerned with a triad of issues involving in each instance both theory and practice — freedom of expression, law, and communication — it is well to pursue our study based on constructions broad enough to include each of these concerns, yet narrow enough to provide for the distinctions among them. Additionally, it is absolutely necessary to develop research criteria in which we recognize not only the overlap of communication, law, and freedom of expression, but that account for the unique characteristics of each. We'll consider the full plethora here in order to clarify and establish distinctions among research functions and types. In doing so we will consider levels of analysis, methodologies, and functions. We will also recognize differences among policy research, applied trial research, and research developed with a primary motivation based in a theoretical context. Our expectations should not be such that we attempt to satisfy all needs with a single study. There are a variety of research functions. Furthermore, while the researcher may design the work to meet the needs of a particular function, circumstance may dictate that the results will be later applied in an unintended manner.

Levels of Analysis

The primary organizational distinction within the very general heading of social science is between macro and micro research. On the micro level we attempt to understand the processes and effects of communication on the individual and recognize that law makes certain assumptions about those effects. The macro level of analysis focuses on the institutional level, and we want to know about the interaction of law with social systems such as journalism.

The level of analysis distinction is especially important as a conceptual distinction in communication and law. We are looking in one instance at law as an institution, then at individuals affected by law, and next at institutions interacting with law. Level of analysis distinctions provide a useful conceptual map for scholars attempting to build communication theory, test legal theory, and then create legal theory.

Communication researchers often use additional levels of analysis. "In social scientific research," writes Earl Babbie, "there is a wide range of variation in what or whom is studied: what are technically called units of analysis."[21] Babbie includes as possible units individuals, organizations, groups, and social artifacts. Berger and Chaffee in *Handbook of Communication Science* identify four basic levels: intraindividual, interpersonal, network, and macroscopic. Usefulness, rather than any hard and fast rule, is the guide.

RESEARCH FUNCTIONS

Research in communication and law may serve any of a number of functions. For present purposes it is useful to distinguish among policy research, applied trial research, and basic theory construction.

Policy Research

Policy research is conducted to determine whether conditions A or B or C will best lead to a desired end. Suppose for example there is agreement that the end we seek is a robust marketplace of ideas through the broadcast media channels. Legislators, citizens groups, and trade associations might *debate* the best way to achieve that end. One group calls for a legislated fairness doctrine. Another throws its influence behind an unregulated economic market. Such debate — very likely infected by economic, political, and other special interests — would benefit from systematic social research that tests each of the competing hypotheses. It may well be that communication research is appropriate. Empirical tools can be effectively brought to bear in this arena. Policy research has obvious application during the legislative process, and it is useful as a means to identify and test the judicial outcome against the desired social or political outcome.

It is necessary to distinguish, however, between general assertions that communication theory does not back up the assumptions that appear to underlie certain policies and research that tests those assumptions in a manner that makes them useful to the debate. An early stage of research or discipline development is the observation that something needs attention. We observe — fairly frequently — that the effects of communication are not as uniform, powerful, and immediate as many lawmakers and judges assume they are. We rarely take the next step. The observation has been made — repeatedly — that communication X might not cause action Y. Yet calls for this recognition continue to a point of annoying redundancy approaching television commercials for products normally used in private. Those interested in policy must now *conduct* communication research that provides hard evidence. To do less continues the policy debate, but does not test the policy and thereby provide information that can inform the debate.

Policy research, at least within the social science context, should be as close to value free as possible. Yet the notion that research is value free is probably close to oxymoronic given the nature of the debates that inhabit freedom of expression policy decisions. The communication researcher must distinguish between the function of the research and the use to which that research may later be put.

We should not expect to control all the ways in which our work will be applied. Neil Malamuth, a communication psychologist at UCLA, found himself in just such a predicament. Some of his work focuses on male attitudes toward women and the ways in which those attitudes have been influenced by mass media — especially media messages conveying sex and/or violence.[22] Malamuth is opposed to censorship, yet found his studies cited in Europe and New Zealand in justification of media restrictions and legislation.

Malamuth did not intend that his work be used to set policy. In fact, he turned down an invitation to be a member of a federal commission on pornography. Yet clearly communication scientists do not live in a value free world and should expect that their work may indeed have policy implications. There are deep wrinkles to this issue in the field of communication and law. For, traditionally, much of the work in freedom of expression and in media law has been value laden. Theorists such as Meiklejohn, Bollinger, Emerson, Kalven, and Blasi have developed First Amendment theories founded on certain democratic rather than scientific values. Where are the responsibilities of the researcher who transverses science and law? Should the communication researcher confront these questions directly each time research is undertaken? Or does such an approach inherently disable the communication scientist from the ability to conduct truly scientific work?

When we talk about policy research it could be material commissioned by a legislature concerned with the effects of laws on communication, or the effects of communication on particular laws. The work might as easily be commissioned by a special interest group such as a publishers' association or a broadcast industry trade association intent on lobbying Congress or a local city council. Very often, policy research is commissioned work—in the language of social science, *applied research*. It may be similar to the applied research presented at a trial, either de novo or interdisciplinary.

Applied Trial Research

We also have referred to applied trial research. By this we refer to studies undertaken to answer specific fact questions in specific trial situations. There are obvious similarities between policy research and trial research. Each attempts to provide social facts. The Wayne Newton libel trial, for example, produced survey evidence purporting to show a loss of reputation caused by the television reports that generated the suit. Social scientific research developed specifically for a court is also referred to as de novo research. We'll examine this concept further below. As the demand for expert witnesses increases it is likely the amount of research generated to fit the needs of legal advocacy also will increase—especially as attorneys seek studies tailored to the specifics of the cases they are prosecuting.

Theory

When we talk about theory we are referring either to legal theory or to communication theory. Research aimed at theory need not take into account the immediate application of arguments to a trial or judicial appeal. Our answer to the question—Why should a court accept communication theory?—is quite simple. It does not matter for our purposes whether or not the courts are inclined to make use of communication research. The individual undertaking applied research may care a great deal. The individual examining theory, however, owes allegiance not to clients or to any other vested interest. Here it is neither clichéd nor trite to suggest that the theorist seeks only knowledge and understanding—and in the case of communication and law we seek understanding about the discipline of communication. How do the workings of various involved institutions affect other institutions? We are concerned not only with how things work, but with how they should work. Here we recognize the overlapping functions in law and freedom of expression.

In our recognition we also come to know that law is indeed a very practical and very results-oriented endeavor. We do not mean to suggest that communication theorists should not also work toward development of legal theory—which may indeed be operationalized in a court of law. Unlike communication theory, legal theory must provide significant coverage. Social scientists have the luxury of time and narrow focus. Legal theorists must work toward differing ends. The communication theorist develops and tests communication theory, questions legal theory where it intersects with the discipline of communication, and may suggest new legal theory based upon communication. We want to theorize about law and about freedom of expression using contextual understanding made possible by communication research.

RESEARCH STRATEGIES

Legal scholars generally recognize three varieties of research under the social science umbrella: interdisciplinary analysis, de novo research, and descriptive analysis. Any of these may be an element in the construction of legal theory or may find use in the development of legislation or in the practice of jurisprudence. Note that these are not research methodologies in the sense of using an experimental design, or a scientific survey. Rather they are strategies for accomplishing particular tasks given the existence of particular data or the requirements of a given situation.

Interdisciplinary Analysis

Researchers and theorists utilizing interdisciplinary analysis apply existing communication research to concrete legal questions or to explorations of legal theory—what law and psychology professor Wallace Loh has referred to as "collating available research information with a legal problem."[23]

A familiar example for communication scholars is provided by much of the research focusing on cameras in the courtroom. The legal question at issue is: Does the presence of cameras in a courtroom inherently deny an individual constitutionally guaranteed rights to a fair trial? The question is framed by the social policy dictated by Anglo-American legal tradition and by the Constitution which establishes principles found in the 6th and 14th Amendments. The constitutional principle — in this case, the right to a fair trial — is operationalized as a social policy that places restrictions on behavior likely to jeopardize the guaranteed right. Related to, but independent of, the social policy, is the question of social facts. Does a particular stimulus — the presence of cameras — within a particular situation — a trial or an appellate hearing — cause directly or indirectly a particular phenomenon — a denial of due process? The fair trial is the *principle* at issue. The inclusion or absence of cameras to ensure that principle is the social *policy*. The actual condition caused by the presence or lack of cameras is the social *fact*.

The debate was brought to the Supreme Court in 1965 in *Estes v. Texas*.[24] Billie Sol Estes, a Texas businessman and personal friend of Lyndon Johnson, was tried on charges of theft, swindling, and embezzlement. He appealed his conviction, claiming the presence of cameras at his pretrial hearing and at portions of his trial violated his right of due process. Chief Justice Earl Warren was outraged. In a draft opinion never actually issued, Warren declared that allowing television in a courtroom was "allowing the Courtroom to become a public spectacle and source of entertainment."[25] Justice Douglas, usually sympathetic on issues with even a remote bearing on the public's ability to monitor the processes of government, called the prospect of televised trials "the modern farce — putting the courtroom into a . . . theatrical production."[26]

Estes produced a Court united in principle. The justices agreed on the basic premise of a defendant's right to a fair trial. But the Court splintered on legal policy, finally producing only a plurality opinion. Did the Constitution prohibit cameras per se as an inherent violation of guaranteed rights? Or was this a matter of ad hoc balancing dependent in each new situation upon the facts at hand? The central fracture was in fact the result of a lack of relevant and agreed upon social facts. Justice Byron White was most succinct. "We know too little," he wrote in a concurring opinion, "of the actual impact [of cameras in the courtroom] to reach a conclusion on the bare bones of the evidence before us."[27]

Resolution came 17 years later in *Chandler v. Florida*.[28] Here, two policemen accused of attempted robbery objected to the presence of cameras at their trial and appealed their convictions. They claimed that the presence of cameras denied their 14th Amendment rights of due process. This time the avowed social policy of the Court remained the same — a fair trial with substantive due process for the defendants — but this time the Court's access to social facts was aided by a growing literature of communication and judicial research. Chief Justice Warren Burger took judicial notice of communication research that was far more sophisticated than anything available at the time of *Estes*. By 1981 the bulk of the available material on electronic news gathering and still photography in courtrooms was united in the conclusion that the presence of cameras at a trial, in and of itself, had no inherent substantive effect on the defendant's ability to receive a fair trial. In a footnote the Chief Justice wrote, "The data now available do not support the proposition that, in every case and in all circumstances, electronic coverage creates a significant adverse effect upon the participants in a trial."[29]

The Chief Justice had been a frequent and vocal critic of electronic courtroom broadcasting, going so far at one point as to refuse to deliver a keynote address to the American Bar Association until the television cameras were cleared from the auditorium. Yet the availability of reliable social facts made it possible to replace the visceral reaction of *Estes* with an outcome seemingly more in line with reality.

Judicial notice, mentioned above as an avenue available to the Court in *Chandler*, deserves special attention. It is a concept that allows a court to take into consideration facts that are not presented in evidence but which nonetheless may be acted upon without further proof. Clearly, judicial notice is one means by which social research may play an important role in the line of reasoning a judge uses to justify the court's written opinion. The most celebrated example is Chief Justice Earl Warren's use of judicial notice in the *Brown v. Board of Education* (1954) desegregation case in which the Court's opinion simply pointed out with references in footnote 11 the psychological harm to black youngsters caused by the legal construct of "separate but equal."[30] The research to which Chief Justice Burger referred was not conducted specifically within the confines of the Chandler trial. Rather, the Court looked at studies about the problem in general and said that, based on the aggregate of available data, a defendant would have to prove that in his/her particular case there was specific damage.

De Novo Research

The Latin term *de novo* in law simply refers to the process of creating something anew, in our case, research directed at a specific legal question. Rather than extrapolation from existing knowledge, social scientists engage in new studies specifically tailored to given legal issues.

Exemplary here is the survey research commissioned by the plaintiff in *Newton v. NBC* (1987), a libel trial in which the entertainer hired a polling firm to establish the harm to his reputation he alleged was the result of defamatory *NBC News* broadcasts.[31] The operationalized legal question of defamation is a social policy question, framed by the Constitution, state and federal law, tradition, and social norms. The social facts necessary to go to the heart of the policy question, however, might better be answered by social scientists than by attorneys. Did NBC's broadcasts have the communication effect of causing individuals to alter their opinions of Newton? If the answer is yes, then it is for the social policy makers to decide whether that effect should place NBC at liability. But the establishment of the social fact that NBC's actions were necessary and sufficient to bring about that effect — harm to Newton's reputation — is a question of social fact and not of social policy.

In truth, this is an oversimplification of the legal concept of defamation. While the communication researcher is concerned with both necessity and sufficiency, the libel attorney need not go so far. The tort of defamation does not require empirical proof of documented reputational damage, only the likelihood of such. Judge Lois Forer stressed that point when she wrote, "We see plaintiffs who have suffered little, if any, harm demanding and receiving huge sums in damages."[32]

VALUES

The notions of bias and values are regularly raised in discussions of science and law. Is scientific research "value free"? Is it tainted by personal or political values carried by the individual researcher or the institutions that make up the community? Values and bias raise particular questions for those interested in communication and law because of the nature of the beast. The discipline of scientific methodology is intended to eviscerate the biases of personal value systems that may creep into a scientist's research. Certainly, communication scientists attempt to adhere to the goals of scientific inquiry, bolstered by rigorous journal and professional association refereeing systems.

Yet freedom of expression defies scientific truth. The Enlightenment may well have proclaimed that it is in man's natural core to be free, to practice freedom of expression. "We believed that man was a rational animal," wrote Thomas Jefferson. "We believed that men, habituated to thinking for themselves, and to follow their reason as guide, would be more easily and safely governed than with minds nourished in error and vitiated and debased by ignorance."[33] Nonetheless, little scientific proof is available today suggesting a natural law that governs our actions in this regard. Rather, First Amendment theory and freedom of expression theory are based upon positivist and libertarian value systems. Law and freedom of expression may be studied by the scientist, but in the end they are not science — at least not in the classical sense of the term.

First Amendment theorists analyze social contexts within the parameters of paradigms no more based on science than is fortune-telling. What special hazards await us, then, when we attempt to mix communication science with values whose arrangements are determined not by the natural laws of physics, chemistry, and biology, but by philosophers and judges and to no small degree the exigencies of history? Where does the responsibility of the researcher lie in communication and law? To scientific inquiry that may challenge the libertarian claims of First Amendment *advocates*? To freedom of expression theory that may fly in the face of testable social *facts*? The answers are not forthcoming. At least not per se. Yet the questions cannot be ignored, and social research in communication and law cannot ignore either the posing of the questions or the consequences of the answers.

NOTES

1. See generally Everette E. Dennis, "Doctoral Education May Be Our Best-Kept Secret," *ASJMC Insights* (1989).

2. Charles R. Berger and Steven H. Chaffee, "The Study of Communication as a Science," in Charles R. Berger and Steven H. Chaffee, eds., *Handbook of Communication Science* (Beverly Hills, Cal., 1987): 18–19.

3. Richard Polenberg, *Fighting Faiths* (New York, 1987); Abrams v. U.S., 250 U.S. 616 (1919).

4. Ibid., 119.

5. Oliver Wendell Holmes, Jr., "The Path of the Law," *Harvard Law Review* 10 (1897): 458.

6. Morris Cohen, *Law and the Social Order* (New Brunswick, N.J., 1982): 185.

7. Ibid., 186.

8. Ibid., 188.

9. Lawrence J. Berman, *Law and Revolution* (Cambridge, Mass., 1983); Cohen, *Law and the Social Order*; Ronald Dworkin, *A Matter of Principle* (Cambridge, Mass., 1985) and *Taking Rights Seriously* (Cambridge, Mass., 1977); Carl Joachim Friedrich, *The Philosophy of Law in Historical Perspective* (Chicago, 1963); H.L.A. Hart, *Essays in Jurisprudence and Philosophy* (New York, 1983).

10. Frisby v. Schultz, 108 S. Ct. 2495 (1987).

11. Cathy Packer, *Freedom of Expression in the American Military: A Communication Modeling Analysis* (New York, 1989).

12. William Haskins, John Patzke, and Michael Price, "Freedom of Speech: A Review Based upon Analytical Communication Models," *Communication and the Law* 8 (1986): 54.

13. Jeremy Cohen and Albert C. Gunther, "Libel as Communication Phenomena," *Communication and the Law* 9 (1987): 30.

14. Jeremy Cohen, *Congress Shall Make No Law* (Ames, Ia., 1989): 87.

15. Steve N. Chaffee and John Hochheimer, "The Beginnings of Political Communication Research in the U.S.: Origins of the Limited Effects' Model," in E. M. Rogers and F. Balle, eds., *Mass Communication in the United States and Western Europe* (1985): 31.

16. Schenck v. United States, 249 U.S. 47, 52 (1919).

17. Harry Kalven, Jr., *A Worthy Tradition* (New York, 1988): 146.

18. David Anderson, "Media Success in the Supreme Court," Gannett Center for Media Studies Working Paper (1987): 4.

19. Ibid., 13.

20. Chandler v. Florida, 101 S. Ct. 802 (1981).

21. Earl Babbie, *The Practice of Social Research*, 5th ed. (Belmont, Cal., 1989): 82.

22. Neil Malamuth and John Briere, "Sexual Violence in the Media: Indirect Effects on Aggression Against Women," *Journal of Social Issues* 42 (1986): 75.

23. Wallace Loh, *Social Research in Law* (New York, 1984).

24. Estes v. Texas, 381 U.S. 532 (1965).

25. Bernard Schwartz, *The Unpublished Opinions of the Warren Court* (New York, 1985): 192.

26. Ibid.

27. Ibid.

28. Chandler v. Florida, 101 S. Ct. 802 (1981).

29. Ibid., 810.

30. Brown v. Board of Education of Topeka, 347 U.S. 483 (1954); see generally Richard Kluger, *Simple Justice* (New York, 1977).

31. Newton v. NBC, 14 *Media Law Reporter* 1914 (1987).

32. Lois Forer, *A Chilling Effect* (New York, 1987): 24.

33. In Henry Steel Commager, *Jefferson Nationalism and the Enlightenment* (New York, 1975): 5.

6

A RESEARCH AGENDA FOR COMMUNICATION AND LAW

Communication and law builds on a long tradition of freedom of expression research. The conceptual map for theory-driven research presented here offers a variety of opportunities to build on that tradition.

The goal of this book is to encourage research in communication and law and to build on a long tradition of research on questions of freedom of expression in journalism and communication departments.

In a *Journalism History* interview published in 1978, Fredrick S. Siebert said that *Four Theories of the Press* (1957), one of the first attempts to fashion theoretical constructs for thinking about free expression, grew out of a seminar Siebert and Wilbur Schramm taught in the graduate program at the University of Illinois. It was intended, Siebert said, to "fill a void, but I didn't think anybody else would be interested."[1]

The history of scholars working in schools of journalism and mass communication(s) filling the void created by a lack of attention to the relationships among law, communication, and freedom of expression is one of which those of us now working in the field should be justly proud and appreciative. While there have been notable exceptions such as those discussed in Chapter 3, only in recent years have law journals and other noncommunication literatures started to pay significant attention to questions of freedom of expression.

The growing involvement of lawyers and legal scholars in the literature is welcome. This book relies heavily on the work of legal writers, but the influence is not all to the good. As one well-known mass media law scholar observed while walking to meet his undergraduate media law class several winters ago, "Mass media law was fun until the lawyers got involved." The professor's complaint concerned the emphasis lawyers place on narrow legal arguments, sometimes at the expense of broader substantive issues.

For decades, the work of scholars such as Siebert, Frank Thayer, J. Edward Gerald, Harold L. Nelson, Donald M. Gillmor, and later, Dwight Teeter and Don R. Pember not only defined the field of mass communication law in communication and journalism schools, but also helped create a foundation literature where none existed. For the most part, they used legal and historical methodologies to address questions of free press history and law. Their concern was protection of freedom of expression. The work was intended to strengthen, through understanding, society's appreciation of the importance of freedom of the press in a democracy.[2] Interdisciplinary social research in communication and law offers the opportunity to build on the foundation of mass media law research and to make a unique contribution to the understanding of freedom of expression.

Unfortunately, the bulk of our literature is composed of studies in which legal method is used to answer legal questions. There is a dearth of writing that clearly distinguishes communication studies from legal studies. There is a rich and ongoing discourse about legal and philosophical theories of freedom of expression. Communication researchers should be active participants in that discourse.

We are not suggesting that communication researchers stop using legal method. To the contrary, we urge communication scholars to use legal method *and* social research methods as tools in the process of building theories of communication and law.

Communication researchers can bring a perspective distinguishable from that of legal scholars to the questions raised in the law of freedom of expression. Scholarship in communication history is one area where the contribution is present. Histories addressing aspects of freedom of the press by communication historians, such as Margaret Blanchard, Jeffery Smith, and Patrick Washburn, make significant contributions to the historiography of freedom of expression by addressing questions that go beyond the narrow legal rules.[3]

It is the presence of communication issues that distinguishes First Amendment speech and press clause questions from other legal issues. Under the broad umbrella of communication studies, the opportunity exists to examine and make sense of free expression as a question of communication and law. We have presented a conceptual map for theory-driven research in communication and law. The major landmark on that map is the need to recognize the differences between the disciplines of law and communication, but at the same time to identify the nexus between them.

The common ground is freedom of expression. In the law, freedom of expression is defined and understood in terms of normative theories about the way in which society should be ordered and the rights a person must have in society. In communication, freedom of expression also involves communication behaviors or phenomena. The task of the researcher in communication and law is to fashion theory that will enable us to understand better the interactions of communication and of law, using observations that go beyond legal case analysis or use of the methodological tools borrowed from political science.

This book is an invitation to challenge assumptions, not a book of answers. The challenge is to understand communication and law without ignoring either communication or law and to find approaches to the study of freedom of expression that incorporate and build on the important conceptual and theoretical work in both fields of study.

This is not an easy task. There are inherent tensions in *both* the communication and legal academic communities. There are core differences among the values of First Amendment advocates working within the dominant paradigm of liberal free expression theory, the researcher striving for value-free empirical research, and the critical theorist challenging both the dominant liberal paradigm and empirical research. As communication researchers interested in questions of freedom of expression, our goal is to prompt communication researchers to begin looking at freedom of expression, not as a question of law or as a question of communication effects, but as a question of communication and law.

The unexamined free expression questions that can be productively studied using a communication and law approach cross the methodological and theoretical boundaries in legal and communication studies. This is not to suggest that the theoretical differences that distinguish the communication scientist from the critical theorist disappear within the domain of communication and law. They do not.

However, there is more than enough room in communication and law for the myriad of research approaches found under the umbrella of communication studies. The goal is to develop a better understanding of freedom of expression. The ferment generated by a variety of communication and law studies using different research approaches will certainly generate heat, and we hope, much light.

What are the kinds of questions open to research under the heading of communication and law? A specific research agenda cannot be dictated and since communication and law is an emerging area of research there are too few examples of existing research. Certainly, we can bring the communication research light to bear on areas such as libel, judicial decision making, privacy, and media regulation questions. We have attempted to suggest a number of different avenues for examination, but by no means do we cover the entire potential spectrum. Our discussion has been defined in large part by our personal research interests. Personal interests shaped by the parameters of communication and law may well lead to a different set of questions.

Our hope is that in shaping questions about freedom of expression you will integrate communication theory into the study of the law of freedom of expression. On the one hand, the lack of a large body of existing work in communication and law presents a problem. Theory construction is easier (not necessarily simpler) when entering ground previously tilled. On the other hand, the lack of existing work presents an uncluttered terrain for creative and useful work.

NOTES

1. Richard A. Schwarzlose, "An interview with Fredrick S. Siebert," *Journalism History* 5 (1979): 106; Fred Siebert, Theodore Peterson, and Wilbur Schramm, *Four Theories of the Press* (Urbana, 1956).

2. Frank Thayer, *Legal Control of the Press* (Chicago, 1944); J. Edward Gerald, *The Press and the Constitution* (Minneapolis, 1948); Harold L. Nelson, *Libel in News of Congressional Investigating Committees* (Minneapolis, 1961); "Seditious Libel in Colonial America," *American Journal of Legal History* 3 (1959): 160; *Freedom of the Press from Hamilton to the Warren Court* (Indianapolis, 1967); Donald M. Gillmor and Jerome A. Barron, *Mass Communication Law* (St. Paul, Minn., 1974); "The Fragile First," *Hamline Law Review* 8 (1985): 277; Dwight L. Teeter et al., *Law of Mass Communications* 6th ed. (Westbury, N.Y., 1989); "The Printer and the Chief Justice: Seditious Libel in 1782–83," *Journalism Quarterly* 45 (1968): 235; Don R. Pember, *Privacy and the Press* (Seattle, 1972), *Mass Media Law* 5th ed. (Dubuque, Ia., 1989).

3. Margaret A. Blanchard, *Exporting the First Amendment* (New York, 1988); Jeffery A. Smith, *Printers and Press Freedom* (New York, 1988); Patrick S. Washburn, *A Question of Sedition* (New York, 1986); see also Patrick Parsons, *Cable Television and the First Amendment* (Lexington, Mass., 1987); Jeremy Cohen, *Congress Shall Make No Law* (Ames, Ia., 1988); Timothy W. Gleason, *The Watchdog Concept* (Ames, Ia., 1990).

INDEX

ABOUT THE AUTHORS

JEREMY COHEN is Assistant Professor of Communication at Stanford University where he teaches coursework in communication and law, media law, and mass media and society. He is the author of *Congress Shall Make No Law: Oliver Wendell Holmes, the First Amendment, and Judicial Decision Making*. He has lectured in Africa and Europe on the role of the press in the United States for the United States Information Agency. His current research on communication and law appears in *Public Opinion Quarterly, Journalism Quarterly, American Journalism*, and in legal journals. Cohen is a member of the editorial board of *Journalism Monographs*. He received his doctorate in communications from the University of Washington.

TIMOTHY GLEASON is Assistant Professor in the School of Journalism, University of Oregon, where he teaches mass media law, journalism ethics, and news-editorial courses. He is the author of *The Watchdog Concept: The Press and the Courts in Nineteenth Century America*. His research is published in *Journalism History, American Journalism*, and the *Hastings Journal of Communication and Entertainment Law*. Gleason is a member of the editorial board of *American Journalism*. He received his doctorate in communications from the University of Washington.

NOTES

NOTES

NOTES

NOTES